EMOTIONAL AND BEHAVIORAL PROBLEMS IN THE CLASSROOM
A Memoir

EMOTIONAL AND BEHAVIORAL PROBLEMS IN THE CLASSROOM

A Memoir

By

HERBERT GROSSMAN, Ph.D.

San Jose State University
San Jose, California

Charles C Thomas
PUBLISHER • LTD.
SPRINGFIELD • ILLINOIS • U.S.A.

Published and Distributed Throughout the World by

CHARLES C THOMAS • PUBLISHER, LTD.
2600 South First Street
Springfield, Illinois 62704

ISBN 0-398-07086-5 (paper)

Library of Congress Catalog Card Number: 00-039212

With THOMAS BOOKS *careful attention is given to all details of manufactur-
ing and design. It is the Publisher's desire to present books that are satisfactory as to
their physical qualities and artistic possibilities and appropriate for their particular
use.* THOMAS BOOKS *will be true to those laws of quality that assure a good
name and good will.*

Printed in the United States of America
PB-R-3

Library of Congress Cataloging-in-Publication Data

Grossman, Herbert, 1934-
Emotional and behavioral problems in the classroom : a memoir / by
Herbert Grossman.
p. cm.
Includes bibliographical references.
ISBN 0-398-07086-5 (pbk.)
1. Grossman, Herbert, 1934- 2. Teachers--United States--Biography. 3.
Classroom management. 4. Problem children--Education. I. Title.

LA2317.G76 A3 2000
371.102'4--dc21

00-039212

To my fabulous wife Suzanne

PREFACE

As you can tell by its title, this is not a "how to" book. It is a memoir of my experiences during the 42 years I taught students with emotional and behavioral problems and trained others to do so. It begins with my first job in 1957 as a high school teacher in a residential treatment center in New York and ends with my most recent position as a teacher trainer in Malawi, Africa.

I have included an abundance of anecdotes from my work with children and adolescents and with students in the departments of regular education, special education, psychology, and psychiatry of 16 universities in the United States, Africa, Europe, and Latin America that I anticipate will help me accomplish two important goals.

Perhaps you remember the story of the blind men and the elephant. Each man was allowed to examine one small part of the elephant. The blind man who examined the elephant's tail reported that the elephant was like a snake. The one who felt its leg said no, an elephant was more like a tree, and so on. Since none of them had the full picture, none of them understood what an elephant really was. When I started teaching I had no conception of the elephant, "teaching students with emotional and behavioral problems." Not having completed a regular education teacher- preparation program, much less a special education program, I hadn't had a chance to explore a single aspect of the elephant. However, I was eager to learn. I wanted to know the whole elephant.

Throughout the memoir I describe the *mistakes* I made at each stage of my learning about the elephant and the misconceptions and misunderstandings I brought with me to the job that caused me to make them. Hopefully, regular and special education teachers and teachers-in-training will be prompted by my experiences to question their beliefs and attitudes about children and adolescents with emotional and behavioral problems and the best ways to educate them. And, by questioning them, they will avoid the kinds of mistakes their individual misconceptions and misunderstandings cause.

Secondly, I describe the *positive* things I have learned as a result of my attempts to grasp the whole elephant by formal studies in clinical psychology, neuropsychology, and the biological basis of behavior, as well as informal explorations of multicultural and gender issues. I also explain the positive things I have learned from my experiences teaching African American, Asian Pacific Island American, European American, and Latino students in the United States, as well as regular and special education teachers and teachers-in-training at home and abroad. I hope that sharing the positive knowledge I have acquired during my 42-year adventure will provide readers with some useful information, models, and shortcuts in their attempts to help students.

H.G.

ACKNOWLEDGMENTS

I would like to express my appreciation to professors Gail Fitzgerald and Louis Semrau whose out-of-the-blue invitation to be the instructor/consultant of an online conference on diversity issues in teaching students with emotional and behavioral problems led to the writing of an early draft of this book.

CONTENTS

EMOTIONAL AND BEHAVIORAL PROBLEMS IN THE CLASSROOM
A Memoir

Chapter 1

MY FIRST TEACHING EXPERIENCE

DURING THE GREAT DEPRESSION of the 1930s, without any kind of diploma or trade, it was tremendously difficult for my father to earn enough to feed us, clothe us, and pay the rent. For nine years, my parents had to make do any way they could. My father had three ways of making money in those days: peddling fruits and vegetables; buying and selling rags, paper, scrap metal, second-hand furniture, and other miscellaneous junk; and the occasional jobs he sometimes secured from the Works Progress Administration (WPA), a federal program designed to provide some employment for the unemployed. Occasionally, he fought a four-round fight at one of the local boxing clubs. My father knew what it meant to want to work and to be unable to do so through no fault of his own.

World War II changed all that. Suddenly, there was a great demand for labor. My father found work on the docks, first as a stevedore, and then as a welder, repairing ships that had been damaged in battle.

When the war ended, my father lost his good-paying job and we moved to the docks of Brooklyn. Sunset Park was the only green area for miles. There was a big, inviting pool in the park that cost ten cents–the same as a round trip carfare to the beach in Coney Island by subway. Since my friends and I were usually dimeless, we had to choose between climbing the pool fence, hopping the subway turnstile, jumping off one of the docks into the polluted East River when no one was looking, or doing without a swim.

3

Doing without and swimming in the river being the least attractive alternatives, they typically lost out to climbing the fence or hopping the turnstile.

There was a neighborhood movie theater, but the quarter it cost was way beyond our means. So we resorted to a number of techniques in order not to miss out on the movies. Sometimes, if we had the dough, we would all chip in and buy one ticket so someone could get in and open the emergency exit for the rest of us. If we couldn't come up with 25 cents, we would arrange for one of the ushers to open the door for us. Occasionally it was necessary to persuade them to cooperate.

We quit sneaking into the movies, climbing fences, and hopping turnstiles when we started earning money. It should have been clear to anyone that most of my friends were good kids. They did what they did only because they had no other way to get what other kids could get legally. My friends knew right from wrong. Their parents had taught them not to steal. At times, however, their circumstances made it difficult for them to put their knowledge into practice. Once they could afford to behave like upstanding citizens, most of them did.

There is another aspect of my life that I have to describe. From the time I started school, people recognized that I was smart. Before I had a chance to get too bored in the neighborhood school I attended, I was skipped from the second to the fourth grade. Later, my school guidance counselor advised my mother that the neighborhood junior high I was scheduled to attend wasn't suitable for someone with my academic potential. However, I could go to a different school if she insisted that I be assigned to a school where they taught Latin. So, I flourished in a junior high that offered a more academic program, while my friends floundered in the local school.

When we graduated from junior high, I attended

Stuyvesant High School, a school for gifted students, an hour subway ride away in Manhattan; my friends walked to Manual Training High School. I took academic, college preparatory courses; they learned how to work with their hands.

One day during my senior year, I was called to the principal's office. I was told to wear a suit to school the next day because I was to be interviewed by a Harvard recruiter. To make a long story short, the recruiter informed me that if I applied to Harvard and was accepted, I would receive whatever financial aid I required. That was an offer I couldn't refuse.

I wanted to be a teacher when I graduated. It was clear to me that I alone among all the kids in my neighborhood had been born lucky. They had no opportunity to get the kind of education that had changed the way I saw the world and understood things. No one was recruiting them for anything except the army. I wanted to help kids, like the ones I grew up with and had left behind on the docks, to get a good education, to do for some of them what Harvard had done for me. I enrolled in the summer session of an experimental teacher-training program. Six weeks later I had a provisional/emergency license and a job teaching students with emotional and behavioral problems.

The school where I started my career served about 50 young elementary school age children, one hundred adolescent males and 50 adolescent females. Originally it had been part of a walled-in facility for delinquent adolescent boys who spent most of their time working on a farm. By the time I started, the walls had been removed; it had become co-educational; and most of the adolescents spent their school time in various shops, learning trades like printing, beauty culture, automotive repairs, and so on. Those who weren't ready for a vocational program were in self-contained classes. Academics were included but not emphasized. My job description wasn't written down. If it had been, it would have read, "initiate an academic program for teenagers in a school where almost no one believes they are capable of studying academic subjects."

My first day as a teacher was a catastrophe. Remember, I had very little training in education and no experience as a teacher. I had only six weeks of teacher training under my belt and there had not been an academic program at the school until then. I thought I was ready. I had prepared three or four weeks of lesson plans for each of my four courses that I thought would wow the students.

The day was organized to fit the needs of the vocational program. There were two 80-minute periods in the morning with a 15-minute recess period between them. The afternoon was the same. The administration had placed the students into my classes by their gender and age-grade equivalent.

My first class was ninth-grade social studies and English. I had eleven boys, all 14 and 15 years old. They came in at nine o'clock. After they took their seats, I asked their names. The first boy said his name was Wyatt Earp. I let that pass. The second one said his name was Wyatt Earp. I let that pass. When the third student also claimed to be Wyatt Earp, I knew I had to do something. I tried a different tack. I picked up the attendance sheet on my desk and took the roll. No one answered to the first four names. Was everybody Wyatt Earp, I asked. They laughed. I laughed too and started again. No one answered. The boys were still laughing. However, the situation had become unfunny to me. The joke seemed to be on me. Rightly or wrongly, I felt like I was caught in a power struggle that I didn't want to lose.

What could I do? I thought a moment, then had an inspiration. It was fine with me, I told them. They didn't have to answer to their names. I would mark them absent and turn the sheet in that way when the attendance officer picked it up. The boys' attitudes changed. They knew that if they were reported as cutting class they would miss recess, which was a co-ed activity most of them looked forward to. I started from the top of the list again and had no problem.

I felt up, since I had been victorious, but also down, since they had forced me into a situation in which I had had to resort to an authoritarian solution. The mood of the class had also changed. I could sense a tension in the air. The boys had tested me and I had emerged in control. That was the upside. The downside was that I had done so by creating an unpleasant environment.

I spent the first part of the period on social studies. That went fairly smoothly as long as I did the talking. The room went silent when I asked them to participate. When it was time for English, I had the students take turns reading out loud. I discovered that having placed the students into the program by their age-grade equivalency, the supervisors hadn't considered their level of functioning. I had illiterate students and students who were reading at grade level and higher in the same class taking the same subject and supposedly using the same textbooks. I didn't know at the time that in the same classes I had students who had been successful in school before they had been institutionalized and students who had been failing for years and hadn't even been to school for a year or more. I also had a few psychotic students, who were out of touch with reality to varying degrees, mixed in with their non-psychotic peers. This proved to be as much of an educational problem as the students' diverse educational backgrounds.

Toward the end of the period I gave out a sheet with my class rules. No one seemed to object to any of them. I thought I had it made. The final activity was a discussion of the homework assignment for the next day, which I had mimeographed and handed out. The bell rang and the boys hustled out at full speed. I looked around the room. Almost to a man, they had left their assignment sheets and textbooks in class.

The principal came to see me after recess just before the start of the next period. He told me that two girls in my next class were afraid to be close to males because they had been raped. "Keep at least ten feet away from them," he advised me. "And don't make any sudden moves in their direction." There were seven girls on the class roster. "How will I know which ones they are?" I asked. "Good question," he answered. "I'll stay and introduce each of the girls to you as they come in."

I taught the same subjects to them with more or less the same results. There were two differences. I had no name problems, and one of the girls in the front row pushed her desk up against mine and made angry faces at me the whole time. I asked her twice to move her desk back and she refused. Thoughts about moving it myself conjured up a tug-of-war between us that I knew I should avoid. I repeated my request two more times to no avail. Having ruled out a possible tug-of-war, I gave up and let her do what she seemed determined to do, hoping that my supervisor would have a solution for me.

When the bell rang, the girls were quick to leave. It took me a while to leave because I wasn't ready to face the world after what I thought had been a fiasco.

When I walked into the dining room, the principal, who also served as the girls' supervisor, and the supervisor of the adolescent boys called me over to their table. I answered their inquiry about how the morning had gone with a non committal "fine". They looked at me doubtfully. They must have been able to read the dejection on my face.

After lunch the 15 and 16-year-old boys came to class. What a disaster! They had copies of the rules I had handed out in the morning and were using them to do exactly what was verboten. I had written "don't open or close the windows without permission"–two of them were doing just that. I had written "don't carve anything on the desks"– that's exactly what another was doing. I had written "don't throw things"–pencils, paper airplanes, paper clips, and all sorts of miscellaneous objects were flying all over the room. Et cetera, et cetera. I was in no mood for jokes and told them so.

About three or four minutes into the class, in the midst of the turmoil and tumult, one of the few boys sitting in their seats raised his hand and asked to go to the bathroom. Since they had just come to class, I thought it was some mischievous ploy and said no. I settled the students down and began teaching. A few minutes later I acknowledged a student who had raised his hand. "Murray peed on the floor," he announced. There was a puddle under the desk of the student who had asked to go to the bathroom. I ignored the whole thing, again hoping that my supervisor would have a suggestion.

Just before the end of the period, I reminded the boys to take their books and assignment sheets with them when they left and told them to show me their books as they left the room. As soon as the bell rang, completely disregarding what I had said, most of them dashed out of the room sans books, as did the girls in the next class.

To avoid the supervisors, at the end of the day I made a beeline for the station wagon that brought the commuting members of the faculty to the train. I wanted their help. However, even more I wanted to avoid telling them what had happened.

Sitting downtrodden on the train on way home, I made a decision. I took the lesson plans and the stupid list of rules I had prepared out of my briefcase and ripped them into confetti. I would have to start again from scratch. I thought about the tactic I had used to get the boys to tell me their names. I felt bad that I had threatened them with losing recess. I should have handled it differently. I should have continued to see the comical side of the situation and continued to treat it as a joke. I had taken the job to educate students, not to be a disciplinarian, not to punish students. I resolved never to punish students again, and I have always lived up to that resolution, as I will explain later.

When I got home, I was preoccupied with thoughts of how little the students knew about social studies, how ill-prepared they were for the curriculum I had chosen, and how poorly I had dealt with the behavior problems they had created. I couldn't do anything, including go to sleep, until I had figured out what I was going to do the next day. I knew that I had to do something to help the students who couldn't read the textbook. But that problem was postponed in favor of planning how to survive the next day.

The next two days I tried unsuccessfully to convince the students to take their textbooks with them when they left school and to bring them back to class when they returned. Those who were going to do the assignments did so and those who were not did not, despite what I said. I had no more success with the girl who continued to press her desk up against mine and to scowl silently at me the whole period. Then I gave up trying to go it alone, and I turned to my supervisors. They told me that since they, like everyone else, had heard about what had been going on in my classes, they had been wondering whether I was going to quit or admit I needed help.

Together we came up with a solution for the homework and textbook problems. For three days they came to the beginning and end of every class I taught. At the end of each class they made sure all the students left with textbooks and at the beginning of class they prevented students who came to class without their books from entering the room. Students didn't have to come to class with completed assignments, only textbooks. True to my resolution, I made sure that they were not punished if they refused to take their books at the end of class or came to school without them. They just couldn't come to class without the price of admission, their textbooks.

The solution worked for many students, at least those who were willing, interested, and able to read the books. Those who didn't want to be in the class in the first place, and those who were unable to function in an academic class because of their emotional problems, changed their programs.

Sometime during that first semester, one of the supervisors admitted that they had assigned many of the students to my classes without consulting them. They had even assigned some students against their will to fill my classes. Next time, he assured me, only students who wanted to be in academic classes would be assigned to me.

We also discussed the illiterate students who wanted to remain in the class. We had no ready solution for their problem. It took two years to solve it.

My difficulties with the female student proved intractable. During my second week at the school, the principal called her into his office and asked her what the problem was. She was pregnant and I was the father, she answered belligerently. He knew that was impossible. I had never seen her nor she me until the first day of class. A medical examination indicated that she was not pregnant, and a psychiatric examination revealed that she was delusional.

Now that I had a group of students who seemed to want to be in my classes (a little less than half of the original group), I had to figure out how to reach them. That took another month or so. In the interim, almost all of the students who were illiterate dropped out, and I lost some others because I was definitely not a good teacher. By the end of the first semester about 60 percent of the initial group of students had left the program, and a few other students had joined the classes.

I could tell that I was doing better. The students in my classes finally seemed to be happy. The two shop teachers who had gloated over my initial failures and who had adopted a we-told-you-these-kids-weren't academic-material-and-didn't-we-tell-you-that-you-have-to-be-tough-with-them attitude toward me had stopped acting haughtily.

The classes were now about half of their original size—about six or seven boys or three or four girls in each one. Since the groups were small and I was teaching the same classes twice, I came up with the idea of combining the male and female classes for the next semester. The supervisors were worried about control issues; I was raring to go. So we did it.

At first there was an influx of students who, although they had no interest in my classes, had jumped at the opportunity to be in class with their boyfriends and girlfriends. Some of them found motivation; most of them, however, soon dropped out.

Some of the students who had been in the classes before they became coeducational changed their behavior patterns. A few well-behaved students, primarily, but not exclusively males, assumed a more delinquent demeanor. They began to challenge me, made jokes that indicated to the others that they really didn't buy everything I was selling and so on. A few of the girls became shy and stopped volunteering answers or participating in class discussions. Looking back at how I responded to these changes, if my memory serves me, the increase in delinquent behavior galvanized me into action, but I hardly noticed or reacted to the girls' withdrawal.

The delinquent behavior diminished significantly after a month or so; I can't recall how long the withdrawal behavior lasted because it didn't bother me enough to pay sufficient attention to it. (I would certainly react differently now.)

My first day was a catastrophe. My first semester was

problematic. My first year was moderately successful, especially if you consider the fact that I didn't really understand my students and most of my ideas were simplistic and naive about who they were, the problems they were experiencing, how their problems affected their learning and behavior, what and how to teach them, and so on. My ideas might have been somewhat appropriate if I had been teaching so-called disadvantaged kids from my neighborhood in Brooklyn. These students, however, had serious emotional and behavioral problems. Let me give you a few examples of the erroneous beliefs I had to correct.

MISCONCEPTION 1. *If students have difficulty learning something and I show them what the problem is and how to solve it, they will want to correct it and will do so.*

I thought my students would welcome my attempts to help them overcome their learning difficulties, and I became frustrated, even angry, when I was rebuffed. At the time I knew, but didn't think about, the fact that we are not all equally capable of facing the truth about ourselves, especially if the truth would damage our self-esteem or make us anxious, fearful, guilty, or ashamed of ourselves. I had never met a person who was always 100 percent ready to face such truths. I knew that from time to time all of us would rather blame some person or outside force for our failures and mistakes; believe that we had no other choice but to do what we did; or convince ourselves that we really had the ability, but just didn't try hard enough. It took me a while to realize that some students with emotional problems, who are more defensive than most people, are much less able to face facts.

My first lesson occurred about two months into the semester. Steve, a 16-year-old in my world history class, was able to read words at grade level but had little understanding of what he read. His rote memory was excellent. However, he had great difficulty in conceptualizing, abstracting, and generalizing. As a result, his abilities to place events in a time sequence or understand things in terms of causes and effects were extremely limited. In other words, he had a thinking disorder.

He was always talking to me about intellectual things in order to cover up his learning difficulties. For example, he skimmed the *New York Times Book Review* section and dropped the names of the authors and books he read about. Even though I asked him not to, he insisted on handing in extra-credit reports that were basically copied paragraphs from the world history text. And, he discussed in great detail his plans for going off-grounds to school the following year and what he would study in college after that.

I understood that he would never accomplish any of his goals until he was able to comprehend what he read and think logically. Realizing that he had to admit his limitations to himself and to me so that I could help him overcome them, I confronted him about his limitations. He continued to deny them and to hide behind his intellectual facade. Finally, I forced him to face his reading problem. I made him read sections from a reading comprehension book and try to answer the prepared questions about the sections. He couldn't do it! Then I had him read passages from our text-book and answer questions about what he had read. He couldn't do that either! Although he was devastated by the experience, I thought that at last I would be able to help him. I assured him that he would be able to overcome his diffi-culties and made up a schedule of individual tutoring ses-sions. I guaranteed him that I would give him the kind of help he needed to study off-grounds and go to college.

On my arrival the next day, I was called into the princi-pal's office. What had I done to Steve, he asked. I described what had transpired. He told me that Steve had become so depressed over the incident, he had tried to hang himself from a tree and would have succeeded if another student hadn't seen him doing it.

Once I understood the role of our defenses, I noticed that many of my students were defensive about their behavior. I saw how many of them blamed others for their own mistakes and shortcomings; failed to see how they contributed to their own rejections and failures; believed that the constructive criticism they received was uncalled for; justified their inappropriate behavior to themselves by a variety of excuses that were obviously spurious to others; adopted a sour-grapes attitude when things didn't work out as well as they hoped, and convinced themselves that it didn't really matter to them or they really didn't need it anyway; decided that they felt too sick or tired to try something that they were afraid they would fail at; believed what they had done was an accident, that it wasn't a big deal, that the other person had it coming because he started it, and so on. I developed a healthy respect for such defenses and learned less threatening/confronting ways to deal with them.

MISCONCEPTION 2. *Students with emotional problems have poor self-concepts. Making sure that students do well in school is the best way to improve their self-concepts.*

Perhaps because I was an educator in waiting, I focused too much on only one aspect of students' self-concepts, what they thought about their ability to learn—if they were smart, stupid, and so on. It took me a while to realize that quite a few of my students were dealing with other kinds of self-concept problems. Some had serious bouts of guilt because they thought that they they were despicable people. Others felt sad and depressed because they believed that nobody could possibly love or respect or want them since they were unlovable. Some of my students had difficulty in class because their fears and anxieties about succeeding in school interfered with their learning. However, many of them had difficulty learning because they were too sad, depressed, or guilt ridden to be able to function in class. Their emotional problems drained away the energy, interest, and desire to learn that they needed to function in class. These students suffered from extreme self-esteem problems. To say that they didn't like themselves would be an understatement. Many hated themselves.

I knew that success in school could be extremely helpful for students who think they are "stupid idiots." However, I didn't realize or even think about the fact that success in school would do very little to counteract thoughts such as "I am an evil, spoiled, selfish, mean person because of the horrible thing I did to my younger brother," or "I deserve to die because of the repugnant sexual acts I committed with my mother," or "I should be punished because I tried to burn the house down to kill my parents." Those students needed something else. And I had not realized that at the time.

MISCONCEPTION 3. *Education is all important in the lives of students with emotional and behavioral problems. Most of their problems can be solved by helping them succeed in school.*

My attitude about students' self-concepts was just one aspect of my notion that educational success was the most important thing my students could experience. I should have known better. Most of you probably have known at least one person who, despite doing well in school or at his or her job, broke down, turned to drugs, or even tried to kill herself or himself. How effective could I be, if before I started a class, someone were to say the following to me? "Dr. Grossman, Maria is extremely depressed and is talking about killing herself because she just found out that her daughter has Lou Gehrig's disease. She really needs your help. Teach a really good class tonight." It's not likely that my good teaching would help her with her problem. It might not even succeed in diverting her thoughts from her daughter's condition.

MISCONCEPTION 4. *Students know why they behave the way they do and they can choose to control their behavior if they wish.*

Like most people, I have not understood why I continue

to do some of the things I wish I could stop doing. I still don't know why I suffer from claustrophobia and fear of heights. Although I know nothing bad can happen to me in an MRI machine, I still need a tranquilizer before I can get into one. Moreover, no matter how much I try to reason with myself, I still get those unwanted feeling whenever I am in situations that trigger them, and I still can't control my reaction to them.

When I started teaching, however, I acted as if my students knew exactly why they misbehaved and could stop doing so if they wanted to. Although I couldn't understand or control some of my own fears, I forgot that when I was in front of my class. I thought I could reason my students out of their fears by explaining why there was nothing for them to be afraid of.

Now I understand that the help I was offering them—encouraging them to get a grip on themselves was insufficient. And I use other approaches like gradual desensitization to relieve them of their fears.

Also like most people, I sometimes lose control of myself when I am angry and say or do things I later regret. Nevertheless, during my first year of teaching, I behaved as if my students could stop and think before they acted, even though they were much angrier than I had ever been. I forgot that sometimes I acted stupidly when my emotions got the better of my intellect and believed that if I helped my students understand that they harmed themselves when they lost control, they could and would behave more constructively.

I forgot that when students are under the sway of strong emotions they may react in ways they can avoid when they are less upset. I forgot that a student who is intensely anxious before a test might need to start working before reading all of the directions in order to relieve her tension by getting started. And I forgot that a student might become so angry at what another student said to him about his religion, his parents, and such that instead of being able to respond in a way that is commensurate with what the other student did, thereby keeping out of trouble, he might have to overreact.

I know better now. Now I offer educators specific techniques such as relaxing students, allowing them to escape situations that they cannot cope with and so on to use with students who, like all of us, sometimes lose control of themselves when they are too upset by strong emotions to control their actions. I also tell educators not to expect perfection because the techniques will only help to a limited degree. After all, I remind them, their emotionally disturbed students wouldn't need their help if they could control themselves all the time.

MISCONCEPTION 5. *Students are rational beings who can be reasoned with sufficiently to correct any misperceptions that cause their learning and behavioral problems.*

When I started teaching, I knew that we all lose our sense of reality at times. Sometimes a noise that, if someone were at home with us, we would recognize as the branch of a tree rubbing against the outside walls, sounds like someone trying to break in when we are alone at night. Waiting for someone who is late, we can think that some of the people who turn the corner or enter the building are that person even though they in no way resemble the individual. Sometimes, rather than feel guilty about what we have done to someone, we feel angry at them for what we incorrectly imagine they have done to us. I knew these things but forgot to apply my knowledge when my students acted that way. I wanted them to control their behavior. I wanted them to act logically all of the time even though I did not.

I wanted all students to listen to my words of wisdon and start thinking rationally, immediately—including the one who believed that I was the father of her non-existent child and the one who would not allow anyone to touch him because he believed that if enough people touched him all of his skin would be rubbed away and he would eventually disappear.

MISCONCEPTION 6. *An astute observer with sufficient information can discover the motivation behind a student's behavior.*

When I started teaching, I thought I knew when my students purposely did things in order to bother or provoke me and when they acted in ways that inadvertently bothered me. And I believed I knew when they were lying to me and when they mistakenly thought they were telling me the truth. I no longer suffer under that delusion.

I also thought that I could figure out why students did what they did. For example, I was sure one of my students who moved his seat and desk way in the back of the room either didn't want to participate in the class or wanted to be as far away from me as possible. Then one day, as I walked behind his desk in order to get something from a closet, he jumped out of his seat and swung at me. It turned out that he believed people were out to get him, and he sat in the back of the room so they could not attack him from behind.

Who could have known that he thought I might attack him? Who could have guessed, without being told by the principal, that two girls in my class that the principal told me to keep my distance from were terrified of men, if he had not told me so? Who could have guessed the reason why my student pushed her desk up against mine and glared at me. I could give you a zillion more examples.

It didn't take long for me to realize that I shouldn't jump to conclusions about my students' motivations and that even when I thought I understood them, I could be wrong.

MISCONCEPTION 7. *Student's behavior is either acceptable or unacceptable, desirable or undesirable. Behavior that interferes with the rights of others or is harmful to others such as calling out without being called on, interrupting, pushing ahead of, hitting, or teasing others is never acceptable. Conforming to school rules, asking for help when necessary, ris-*

ing to educational challenges, sharing, and cooperating with others are acceptable and desirable behaviors.

When I started teaching, I believed in absolutes. Now I realize that when we are working with students with serious problems there is no absolute standard for judging their behavior. I didn't realize this my first year of teaching and made a number of mistakes. I'll give you two examples.

Lenny was a brilliant student. However, he never said anything in class; never even acknowledged a comment or question directed to him; and spoke as little as possible out of class. About three months into the year, when we were studying the middle ages, totally out of context he suddenly shouted out, "Send the niggers back to Africa."

I had no idea where his remark came from. It wasn't related to anything we had been discussing. I felt that I could not allow him to make such a racist remark without challenging it. After I reprimanded him, he didn't speak again. True enough, his remark was more than unacceptable. On the other hand, his contribution was a first for him. He had said what was on his mind. Perhaps he was beginning to feel comfortable in class. If I had the opportunity to react to his statement again, I hope I would focus on trying to make him feel that it was safe for him to speak in class. I hope I would react in a way that would encourage him to speak his mind, whatever was in it. I hope I would congratulate him on speaking in class and pass on dealing with the derogatory racist content of his comment.

A few weeks later, when Howie did his thing in class, I hadn't learned my lesson yet. Howie was the campus scapegoat who did absolutely nothing to protect himself against the teasing, taunting, and downright cruelty of some of the other students. He was constantly victimized by others, despite the staff's best efforts to protect him. We were in the middle of a class discussion. Someone was teasing Howie right under my nose without me noticing it. Suddenly,

Howie jumped up, let out a scream that they probably heard across campus, picked up his chair, and hurled it at another student. Fortunately, Howie wasn't very strong and the chair fell well short of its mark. I instantly reprimanded Howie for his dangerous behavior and for not reacting in a measured way. I was too upset by Howie's behavior to remember that it was the first time he had defended himself. Instead of reprimanding him, I should have congratulated him on finally standing up for himself.

How could he have responded in a measured way? He was like steam under pressure that finally exploded. He had no experience in expressing anger in an acceptable way. Who had shown him how to do so? Who had helped him practice acceptable ways of standing up for himself? I should have congratulated him first and then later taught him how to respond in a less-intense and less-dangerous manner.

I studied the aggressive behavior of the boys at the school for my doctoral dissertation. As other people's research and my experience had suggested, I found that in certain cases, aggressive behavior can be a positive factor. My research indicated that in many cases, boys who had responded aggressively, even extremely aggressively, to their parents' physical, psychological, or sexual abuse were more likely to have a successful adjustment to life after they had received psychological help than boys who had acquiesced to and accepted the abuse without a struggle.

I was much less naive when I started my second year of teaching. As a result, the program was so successful that at the end of the year the administration hired a math and science teacher to complement the social studies and English classes I taught. I also finished my masters degree program which meant I had learned whatever I was going to learn about teaching from my education professors.

Fortunately, I continued to learn from my colleagues at the school. There were some really great teachers and supervisors on the staff. Their suggestions and insights, based on the practical knowledge they had gained from working with students, were extremely helpful. For other teachers, however, teaching had become, or perhaps always had been, just a job they did until it was time to go home. I didn't appreciate many of their suggestions and ideas. I was trying to correct my naive and simplistic notions about the students; these teachers were comfortable with theirs. I tended to overestimate my students; they underestimated them. I wanted to increase students' intrinsic motivation to learn and behave appropriately; they were content to employ external motivation to get students to conform to their expectations. I was opposed to any kind of punishment; they punished students unnecessarily and often unfairly.

A number of these teachers had allowed their use of power to corrupt them. Using their power to compel their students to do their bidding, they had little reason to improve their instructional and classroom management approaches. And although they were poor teachers, they retained their jobs because they kept their students under control. A couple of them were downright mean. I remember when a teacher who had told a student that he owed him three minutes for coming late to class stopped him just as he was mounting the school bus to go on a class trip. He took the three minutes owed him starting from the time the bus left the campus. The student owed him three minutes, but he ended up losing a full day trip.

A few other teachers and I objected to the staff's use of peer pressure to obtain students' compliance. For example, the coed recess would be delayed until every single student who had lost recess reported to the recess- deprivation room. If even one student failed to show up, the recess would be delayed or canceled. Peer pressure was enough to insure that most students reported on time. However, during my years at the institution, quite a few students paid a very high price for causing recess to be delayed or canceled. If something worked, most members of the teaching staff had few qualms about using it. Not all of us were that way.

Later, when I had learned more about what other teachers and programs were offering students in the 1950s and early 1960s, I realized that with the few exceptions I have mentioned, my colleagues were actually ahead of most teachers in the field. They had merely lacked specialized training and exposure to other ideas. Nowadays there are quite a few teacher-preparation programs that help teachers understand their students from a psychological point of view. That was not the case then.

I wanted to learn more about my students. The practical knowledge I had gained from the good teachers was super. However, I drew a blank when I asked them how the students' emotional problems affected their learning and behavior. Even the really good teachers knew very little about the psychology of their students. They interacted with the clinicians on staff, but they did not feel a need to understand much of what they knew. This may have been because there wasn't a team approach. Each discipline worked separately. The teachers educated the students and the therapists dealt with their psychological problems. In such a situation, it made sense that most of the teachers believed that good teaching alone was enough for them to succeed at what they were doing. However, I wanted to know more. Therefore, I enrolled in a doctoral program in clinical psychology.

At the end of my third year, the administration hired three more teachers. An English teacher enabled me to concentrate exclusively on social studies. A new science teacher permitted the other teacher to focus on his area of expertise, math. And a generalist worked primarily with high-potential low-reading students.

My fourth year was probably the most productive in terms of my personal growth. For one thing, I was permitted to set up an academic program for some of the "organic kids," (brain damaged, mildly developmentally disabled students with emotional problems). This experience helped me to understand how the intellectual problems of developmentally disabled students affect their learning and behavior and how to help these students achieve at their level despite their disabilities.

Secondly, my classes in clinical psychology had helped me finally get a theoretical grasp on how emotional and behavioral disorders can cause learning and behavior problems. And I began to spend two hours a day, three times a week working individually with students after school. Working with students individually enabled me to understand on a practical level the specific ways in which emotional difficulties affect students' learning and behavior. Let me cite a few examples.

I learned to appreciate why students had difficulty learning and behaving appropriately when they were experiencing intense feelings of anxiety, fear, anger, depression, and so on. I could recognize the anxiety that drove insecure students to try to get on my good side by flattering me, asking to do errands for me, handing in extra-credit reports, et cetera, so I would not confront them with their imagined inadequacies. It made sense to me that students who were afraid that people would think they were crazy if people knew what they thought, would resist expressing their opinions, talking about themselves, or writing anything creative. When angry students with chips on their shoulders misinterpreted my actions as insults or infringements on their rights and reacted belligerently, I could understand where they were coming from.

I was able to see how strong emotions could make students distort and misperceive things and how their misperceptions could cause them to behave problematically. It made sense that suspicious, fearful students who believed the world was a hostile and dangerous place, had to keep on guard against potentially dangerous people. Naturally, some of them had to try to provoke me into acting nasty and arbitrary when they were tempted to trust me. They needed me to confirm their belief that it is unwise to trust anyone. It was reasonable then, with some students, that the nicer the teacher, the nastier their behavior.

Students' self destructive behavior was beginning to make sense to me. I understood that in most cases students weren't out to harm themselves; they just ended up doing so. Thus, extremely anxious students didn't want to get the wrong answer or choose an incorrect solution to a problem. It was just that they became so anxious while trying to deal with the challenge, that they chose any answer or any solution, in order to get the situation over with. Although they seemed to purposely attempt to fail by not trying, that wasn't the real cause of their self-defeating behavior. Rather, afraid to risk their self-concepts by trying their best and failing, they made half attempts to succeed. That way, when the expected failure occurred, they could tell themselves, "There is nothing the matter with me. I could have succeeded if I had tried harder." Unfortunately, by leaving themselves an out they helped guarantee that they would fail.

Defensive students also became easier to understand. Of course students who were dealing with overwhelming amounts of guilt about their imagined or real sins would try to keep any possible guilt about their bad behavior out of consciousness by blaming others for their actions. Understandably, students who would feel guilty about not doing something might conveniently forget or repress something that they had to do. That way, they could believe that they had not decided not to do it, but merely forgotten to do it.

I also had some budding understanding of the psychotic thought processes that caused students to grossly misunderstand the world. The thought processes of the student who looked at the map on the wall and concluded that all rivers flow south because water flows downhill and south was at the bottom of the map made sense to me. So did those of the student who tried to push me down a flight of stairs because his uncle, who was named Herbert Gross, abused him repeatedly, and those of the student who would not allow anyone to touch him because he believed that all of his skin could be rubbed away.

I appreciated the fact that we teachers sometimes misunderstand our students' behaviors. For example, some students who appeared to their teachers to be unwilling to behave in a certain way were actually unable to do so because of their emotional problems. And I recognized that we may also take our students' behaviors too personally and mistake the effect their behaviors has on us as the motivation for their behavior. For example, when we are upset by the things students do, we may mistakenly think that students purposely behave that way in order to upset us.

However, the more I understood my students' emotional problems, the more frustrated I felt about those of my colleagues who thought good teaching alone was sufficient. That was one of main reasons I started writing my first book. (1) In it, I attempted to pass on to teachers-in-training what I had learned about how to use psychological insights like the ones mentioned above to better instruct students and manage their discipline problems.

To sum up, I went through three phases as an educator. In the first phase, I assumed that good teaching and classroom management were sufficient. In the second phase, I learned to adapt my instructional and classroom-management techniques to my students' emotional and behavioral problems so they could succeed in school despite their problems. When I reached the third phase, I believed that teachers could and should play an important role in changing students. Rather than merely helping students succeed in spite of their problems, teachers could also contribute to the elimination of the causes of their problems.

I had little opportunity to use changing techniques with students during my years at the school. The school wasn't set up for that. Even when I returned to the school as a clinical psychologist, my role was still very restricted. However, I was about to get a lucky break that would enable me to put into practice the ideas I had about how educators could help change students.

I cannot end this section without also discussing an unpleasant aspect of those years—my initial tip-of-the-iceberg experiences with prejudice and discrimination in education. I'll describe two examples of the tip.

Somewhere around 90 to 95 percent of the students in the school were European Americans; considerably fewer than ten percent were African Americans or Latinos. When, and it wasn't very often, a white female would pair off with a black male, the educational and clinical staff would discuss the diagnostic implications of her behavior. For most of my colleagues, there were only two possible reasons for her behavior. Either she was rebelling against society by breaking a sacred taboo or she felt too inferior to believe that she could attract a white male. Very few staff members could conceive of the possibility that she just liked her black boyfriend.

Have things changed since then? You be the judge. Ask yourself these three questions. What assumptions would a group of European American teachers make about the reasons why an African American high school student would hang out with a group of European American students? Now ask yourself what assumptions they would make about the reasons why a European American male student would hang out with a group of African American male high school students. Finally, ask yourself what they would think about a

European American female student who hung out with a group of African American male students.

During my years at the school there was only one teacher of color. He was a very tall, very well built, very strong, and very handsome African American. The students were attracted to him because of his good looks; his excellent teaching; his calm, relaxed, and soothing manner; and his willingness to make himself available to them when they needed a friend. He is one of only two friends I have kept up with throughout my life. In short, the guy is great.

After his second year his contract was not renewed. Although the administration gave the staff a phony-baloney reason for his dismissal, many of us believed he was let go because the European American white administration was uncomfortable about his close relationship with the female students. I guess it was predictable that a staff that couldn't accept white girls having black boyfriends would not be able to accept their having a therapeutic or friendly relationship with a black man. The irony of the story is that while he always maintained a professional relationship with students, two European American white male staff members, one teacher and one therapist, married students, and two white male non-professional staff members were fired because they abused male students.

This kind of prejudice isn't quite as virulent today as it was in 1961. However, it does rear its ugly head much more than many people are willing to admit.

Chapter 2

NEW YORK CITY

THE DIRECTOR OF THE AGENCY that ran the school where I taught was a pioneer. So it was natural that he would be in the forefront of the movement to deinstitutionalize people away from residential settings and would establish what he said was the first experimental day-treatment program for adolescents who were traditionally placed in correctional facilities, residential treatment centers, or mental hospitals (a kind of harbinger of the least-restrictive setting movement of recent years). When he proposed the idea, the senior educators and clinicians in the agency argued about which profession should be in charge. The educators argued that since it would be a school, it should be run by an educator. The clinicians countered that it would be a treatment center and should be directed by one of their own. They compromised on me, since I belonged to both camps.

The director was wonderful to work for. During our last conversation before the school opened he said to me,

Remember, society considers the boys you will be working with incorrigible, the bottom of the barrel. People are afraid of them—which is the main reason why they are removed from the community. No one can say for certain that they should not be placed in residential settings because they have never been treated any other way. So forget about what is usually done in the field. Try whatever you want. Be as innovative as you want. Just one thing. Don't take too many chances. If some of the boys are too

29

dangerous to keep in the city, don't hesitate to send them to a residential center or hospital. You do not have to succeed with all of them. This is just a pilot project. Find out what things work. See if the program is successful. Remember you do not have to keep every boy you accept. No one is assuming that all the institutions can be closed overnight.

What a perfect job description for someone who likes to do his own thing. I was his man.

We opened the Phoenix School in January 1965. At that time, in New York City and elsewhere, European American emotionally disturbed and delinquent teenagers, especially if they were middle class, typically remained in their communities and were seen by psychotherapists or sent to residential treatment centers. African American and Latino teenagers, on the other hand, were much more likely to be sent to correctional facilities and or psychiatric hospitals. As a result, most of the boys in the program were very poor students of color.

The boys were literally incarcerated and awaiting placement in correctional facilities, residential treatment centers, or mental hospitals. Once we accepted them, instead of being shipped to the facility they were assigned to, they went home and attended our program during the day.

Most of the students had severe emotional problems. One had a conduct/behavior disorder, meaning that he hadn't internalized the moral or ethical principles necessary to control his antisocial impulses. (A number of African American students came to us mislabeled as conduct disordered. Eventually we came to understand that they had been mislabeled by prejudiced assessors who were intolerant of certain behavior patterns that tend to characterize many poor African American males.) And a couple of students were none of the above. They were just extremely poor kids who stole things. However, unlike the ones who got away with it, they tended to be too immature and inept to steal without getting caught.

Approximately two thirds of the 30-some students that entered the program while I was the director were Latino and African American. All but one of them came to us with I.Q. scores that would have qualified them for a program for the developmentally disabled (mentally retarded). All of the European American students had normal or higher I.Q. scores.

As you might expect, none of the so-called retarded students was actually retarded. True, some of them were illiterate to the point of not recognizing many of the letters of the alphabet. However, if they actually had been retarded, they would not have been able to learn as much as they did once they received an appropriate educational approach, and they sure wouldn't have been able to outsmart us as often as they did.

The program we developed at the school can be summarized in six principles. (1)

1. The most important concept was empowerment. We wanted to convince our students that they could achieve their goals, control their behavior, and meet the challenges that confronted them, because they themselves had the power to shape their destinies and futures. To empower our students, we needed to demonstrate our conviction that they could and would control their own behavior. This meant helping them to do so without making them dependent on excessive or unnecessary teacher praise, assistance, or supervision.

We certainly were concerned about the way they behaved in school, but we knew that the tests of our efforts were how they behaved when they were not in school and how they would function after they had left the program. That necessitated downplaying the role of extrinsic motivation and increasing and relying as much as possible on their intrinsic motivation. It required trying to change the students, not merely managing their behavior. This meant emphasizing self-management techniques over teacher-management techniques, when it was necessary to manage them, since teacher management can lead students to believe that they are unable to manage themselves. As one author has put it,

> Perhaps one of the most overriding criticisms of externally oriented management techniques is the tendency of teachers to use these approaches as control tactics, rather than teaching students to become self-directing individuals. Many otherwise-promising teachers resort to interpreting and utilizing traditional management approaches as control tactics, which then results in making students behaviorally stifled, docile, over compliant, and further doubt their abilities. (2)

We tried our best to eliminate extrinsic rewards, since routinely and unnecessarily rewarding students may teach them to strive to please others rather than to accomplish their own internal motives, thereby contributing to their helplessness. Stressing intrinsic rewards, such as students feeling proud of themselves and reaping the benefits of their accomplishments, has the opposite effect. As I said earlier, I was totally against punishing students. Emotionally disturbed students are often unable to behave in ways teachers prefer because of their anxiety, fear, depression, anger, et cetera. Punishing them for not doing so would be extremely unfair and unproductive. In addition, punishment can make students afraid, resentful, and rebellious, which was the way many of them already reacted to school. Of course, negative consequences were necessary. People cannot be relied on to pay their full taxes, park only in designated areas for only designated time periods, and so on if there are no repercussions for not doing so. We needed to have consequences for their behavior. However, we limited ourselves to the logical consequences of their behavior. Thus, if someone was extremely disruptive in class, they had to leave the class rather than interfere with other students' learning. They would never lose part of their allowance, a recreational trip or a privilege that was unrelated to the particular undesirable behavior. We shunned arbitrary consequences like the plague.

2. Individualization was probably the second-most-important concept. Every attempt was made to provide each student with an individualized educational and therapeutic program. Each student was a unique individual. A number of our students had learning disabilities. Some had difficulty learning because of their emotional problems. A few psychotic students had problems learning because their thinking processes were extremely illogical. Some students had no learning problems, but didn't function well in school because of a conduct disorder. And some students had no learning problems whatsoever. Clearly, different students required different instructional and classroom-management approaches.

We had a few very bright students who had been doing well or at least acceptably in school for many years until they developed problems that interfered with their functioning in school. When they overcame their problems, they would be able to go back to learning without any outside assistance. Therefore, school in a traditional sense was not so important for them. Quite a few of our students had learned a great deal at home and in the street. However, despite attending school for eight, nine or ten years, they were still unable to recognize all 26 letters of the alphabet. These students were so far behind that, without an education, they were doomed to a life of misery in this society. Remedial and, in some cases, special education were extremely urgent for them. One of the psychotic students had done well in school until he had become psychotic. He would be able to continue his education without our help once he was able to function rationally. Two other students had been psychotic for many years. They had not learned how to think logically and understood very little of the world around them. They needed us to help them to learn how to think logically. We also had to help them fill all the gaps that existed in their understanding of the world because of the illogical ways they had come to misunderstand things.

Therefore, we designed an individualized educational program for each student. In most cases it was possible to place a group of students in classes together. However, when students needed to work one on one, either the staff did it or we looked for volunteers or student teachers to work with them individually.

The teachers we hired for the program were excellent. They were highly motivated. They prided themselves on the good relationships they had with their students, the excellent feedback they had received from them, and so on. They were raring to go. However, they were not permitted to teach students who were illiterate or who had serious learning problems until they could explain two things. The first one was why the students had not learned very much despite having attended school for many years and, in some cases, having been in special education programs for most of that time. In addition, they had to describe what specifically they were going to do differently so that the students would learn in our program.

The same applied to the teachers' classroom-management approaches. Like me when I had first started teaching, they thought the students needed to learn how to behave. We reminded them that the students had probably been lectured about their behavior a million times so they certainly knew what kind of behavior was expected in school. We discussed the probability that the students had been punished in one way or the other for misbehaving, and they agreed about the futility of using the same punitive approaches again with them. Then we insisted that they not do one more time what other teachers had already tried unsuccessfully. As was the case in the instructional area, they could not intervene when students misbehaved, unless the behavior was dangerous to the student or to others, until they could describe what they were going to do that was different and why it might work.

3. We expanded the traditional role of the educator in many ways. For example, students who were too threatened by the idea of talking to a "shrink" were encouraged to discuss their problems with whichever staff member they felt comfortable with. Some students used teachers as surrogate therapists. Others used them as surrogate parents and worked out with them issues around lack of love and acceptance and dependency.

4. We attempted to provide a non-threatening environment for students. Two different environments were maintained. The first floor looked like an indoor recreation center with a gym, basketball court, pool table, shop, art room and, music room. Students who were extremely threatened by school or too upset to attend school on a particular day could remain on the first floor as long as they wished. The second floor included the classrooms and tutoring offices. This floor served the students who were capable of applying themselves to academic learning tasks and to conform to the demands that the learning situation imposed on them. Some boys waited weeks before they had their first look at the second floor.

Tests, grades, and other symbols of failure were eliminated. Assessment consisted of finding out what a student had or had not learned, or how far he had progressed toward achieving *his own* goals.

Informal relationships between students and staff were encouraged. In most cases they were much less threatening than formal ones.

Students' defenses were respected. We did not try to tear down the defensive walls most of the students had built up against becoming aware of their feelings of helplessness, dependency, and inadequacy (as I had done when I first started teaching). Instead, we concentrated on eliminating their need for them.

5. We provided for the students' basic necessities–food, clothing, entertainment, and so on. The students had enough to deal with in order to overcome their personal problems without having to worry about where they would get carfare, food, and the like. Besides, most of the students, especially the poorest ones, needed financial help from us if they were going to get by without resorting to illegal means.

6. We put into place a process whereby we helped each other deal with the personal problems that were triggered by our interactions with the students. In other words, we tried to get rid of, or at least control, the buttons that the students pushed so we could focus on helping students, not ourselves, in difficult situations. When, despite our best efforts, we became too upset to handle a situation in a calm, thoughtful, rational manner we had to walk away from it and if necessary call someone to handle it for us whose buttons did not get pushed in that situation. The guiding principle was to do nothing, rather than the wrong thing, unless the situation was dangerous.

One of the main difficulties we would face implementing these principles was our lack of experience with students of color. I had almost no experience with African American and Latino students and I had been unsuccessful in my attempts to hire non-European American staff members. Therefore, we were going to have to learn about how the different life experiences, beliefs, values, customs, and strengths of our African American and Latino students affected their learning and behavior and how to adapt our educational and psychological approaches to their cultural and socioeconom-

that we could live with.

We had little experience in dealing with the ethnic and skin-color issues, the resentments, suspicions, fears, misunderstandings, and so on that occurred between us as white staff members and our students of color and their parents. As a result, we made quite a few mistakes until we learned to recognize and resolve them. Here is an example of a mistake we made.

Early in the program, we bought one of our students, Lonnie, a pair of pants to wear for a special occasion. The next day he came to school with a black eye. It turned out that his father had become enraged about the pants, punched him, and used them to stuff up a leaky pipe. Outraged, Lonnie's therapist visited his father at home that evening. His father turned out to be a very hard-working, single parent who was doing his best to support and care for three kids on a very meager salary. Along come these white professionals with their deep pockets. They buy his son something he would like to get for him, but can't afford. Not only do we put him down in front of his oldest son, we also leave him to deal with two jealous kids who want someone to buy them something too. We didn't condone Lonnie's father's behavior. However, we had to admit that our actions had played a major role in creating the problem. We never made that particular mistake again. After that, we tried to help the boys' parents care for their own sons, if they were capable of doing so. And we didn't forget the students' siblings.

I had considerable experience overcoming the initial mistrust and anger that many students with emotional and behavioral problems have towards teachers and other authority figures. However, overcoming the additional mistrust, suspicion, and hostility many of the students of color had towards whites was new to me. It turned out that the same approach that worked with white students—treating students as individuals, satisfying their needs, and respecting them, was just as effective with students of color. I will never forget the day a graduate of the program, who had been extremely suspicious of our motives when he entered the program, made a special trip to see us. Don't go to Harlem on such and such a day, he told us; don't ask him why, just don't go. Sure enough, there was a lot of violence that day in Harlem. It would not have been a good day to make home visits.

I had learned something about helping students resolve their conflicts about being a good student, but I had no experience in working with students who had conflicts about "acting white." The parents of one of our African American students actually held up middle-class whites as models for him to emulate. Hating his parents and resenting their expectations, he had taken his anger out on white authority figures and elementary-school-age white children prior to entering our program. When he first started the program, he experienced behaving well as giving in to his parents demands and as acting white, neither of which were acceptable to him. Fortunately, his anger and resentment was only "skin deep."

Many teachers are afraid of aggressive teenagers. Aggressive teenagers of color tend to be even more frightening to white teachers. Helping the two teachers in the program who were afraid of African American and Latino students to recognize and come to terms with their fears was challenging. The teachers were more comfortable about admitting to themselves that they were afraid of aggressive white males than they were of admitting the same thing about aggressive black males. Here's a "for instance."

During the second year of the program a new European American teacher observed an argument between two African American students she was supervising. Unfamiliar with the behavior of many working-class African American males, she attributed a level of anger to them that would have been correct for the European American students she had worked with in the past. Assuming that they were much angrier or upset than they actually were, she became frightened and concerned that things were about to get out of hand. She told them to calm down, but they told her to be cool because nothing was going down. That incensed her. Now she was afraid and angry. She shouted for help. Two of us rushed in a few seconds later. She was trembling. The boys had been about to get into a fight, she insisted, and had been fresh when she had tried to bring the situation under control. She wanted us to do something about what had happened. She wanted us to teach them a lesson. They told a different story.

Having worked with other African American students for a year and a half, and aware of her lack of experience with them and the kinds of mistakes European American teachers tend to make with African American students, it seemed to us that she had overreacted to a nothing incident. Later in the day, when we explained the situation to her as we understood it, she got angry at us. How did we know what had happened, she fumed. We hadn't been there.

It took a good while before she felt comfortable with the aggressive and intensely emotional way some of the African American students spoke and behaved. Once she did, she became a pro. Toward the end of the school year, a similar situation arose in the gym while she was supervising a basketball game. One of the male teachers thought the two students were about to fight it out and got between them. She became infuriated. "Nothing was going to happen," she protested. "I had the situation under control. You macho guys are always trying to come to my aid. I can handle things myself, thank you."

Why do many white teachers fear black teenagers? Here's my opinion. One reason is that people, including European American teachers, fear the unknown. Secondly, black teenagers tend to express their feelings more intensely. As one author has put it,

> Whites want social interaction to operate at an emotionally subdued level. To realize this goal they first establish the rule that expressive behavior shall be subdued, which develops sensibilities capable of tolerating only relatively subdued outputs . . . Black cultural norms desire levels of public interaction that are more emotionally intense. Consequently they allow individuals to express themselves at the level at which feelings are felt. (3)

And finally, European American teachers are also aware of the ways in which African Americans, Latinos, and poor people are treated by our society. They know about the unemployment, poverty, racism, discrimination, and so on that these students and their families experience. They sense the resentment, anger, and mistrust these students harbor towards the European American establishment that treats them so unjustly. And they are well aware of the periodic angry explosions that have rocked our society when these groups could not take any more. Is it any wonder that down deep they are afraid of how their students may react to them?

The teacher who was afraid of the black students also had difficulty getting her wishes across to them. Her style was to ask, not tell, students to do things, and to speak indirectly rather than directly to them. Instead of *telling* students directly to do something, she would ask, wouldn't you like to, or don't you want to, or don't you think you might find it helpful to learn, pay attention, keep quiet while someone else is talking, et cetera. Because of the non-authoritative way she spoke to them, most of the black students didn't take her seriously. They didn't understand that when she asked them if they thought they should do something, she really wanted and expected them to do it. They behaved much better once she began to speak to them in a more direct and authoritative manner.

I'll mention one more example of the mistakes we made with the African American students before I turn to the Latino students. We didn't know about the important supportive role the church played in the African American community. One day, a student's parole officer called the school to check up on him because he had been told that the boy had run away from home. If that was the case, the parole officer explained, the student would have to go to a correctional facility, because he could not live on his own. The student told us that members of his church had found him a family to stay with and were supervising him. We spoke with church officials who confirmed the student's story. Then we persuaded his parole officer to allow him to remain in our program while he was supervised by church officials. The parole officer doubted that it would work, but then again, he had his doubts about our program as well.

The female teachers and some of the "well-brought-up" male teachers had difficulty dealing with the way the Latino students and a couple of the other students related to the girls they came into contact with on trips or passed in the street. The teachers were used to being treated by or treating members of the opposite sex "more respectfully" than our boys did. When the boys passed "piropos" (compliments said to females who one does not know, about how great they look or how sexy they are), the teachers felt embarrassed and angry that the boys behaved like that while under their supervision. They didn't think about the fact that males and females express interest in one another in different ways in different cultures. They didn't realize that what they considered an insulting form of attention or show of interest, the boys had learned was acceptable.

Most of the staff eventually were able to allow the students to be themselves. However, one of the female teachers was so embarrassed, uncomfortable, or offended (I never understood which one) by their piropos, that even though she realized that their behavior was acceptable in their neighborhoods, she exacted a promise from them that they wouldn't say anything to girls in the street while they were with her.

One of the female teachers had fewer disciplinary problems with the African American students than some of the new male teachers because she had taught elementary school in a black neighborhood. However, she was extremely frustrated and angry that a couple of the Latino students gave her a hard time for no other reason than she was a woman. As one author puts it, "Without stereotyping, one should be conscious of a male Chicanos' lack of understanding in trying to take orders from a female teacher. He will really look up to or listen with better interest if an adult male is talking to him. This youngster is accustomed to following the authoritative rules of a male household figure." (4)

Unfortunately, none of us realized that cultural factors were influencing the way the students were relating to her. We made all kinds of suggestions that had little or no effect on the problem until the Latino students decided on their own to accept her role in the school.

Latinos are expected to be sensitive to the needs, feelings, and desires of others so that it is unnecessary for others to be embarrassed by having to ask for their assistance in a direct manner. Coming from traditional backgrounds, our Latino students were reluctant to ask their teachers or others for help. During the early months of the program, with no Latinos on the staff, we sometimes had difficulty tuning in to one of our Latino students when he needed help but couldn't ask for it in a way that made it obvious to us.

We had grown up in a culture in which people are required to admit when they are wrong or have made a mistake. Our Latino students were brought up in a different culture. They were no less willing to accept the consequences of their behavior as the European American students I had worked with, but they resisted owning up to it. It took us a while to realize that in some cases it was more effective to permit them to save face by not having to admit their errors and mistakes to us.

We wanted our students to become self-confident and self-directed individuals. So when students asked us what we wanted them to work on, we answered, "What do you want to work on?" And when they asked us if the things they made in the shops were good, or if their artistic endeavors were pleasing to the eye, we tended to turn the question back to them by asking them what they thought of their work.

This approach was tolerated and eventually appreciated by the majority of the European American and African American students. However, it didn't work with the Latino students. They were used to receiving a great deal of guidance from adults, feedback about how they were doing, and statements of approval, smiles, pats on the back, and so on when they did something well. Providing the Latino students with less than their customary amount of feedback and praise was so problematic, we had to dispense with the approach.

We also had some communication problems with the parents of the Latino students, not because of language differences, but because of differences in communication styles. We expected the parents to be honest with us, for example, to say whether or not they understood our suggestions about how to deal with some of their sons' problems, whether they agreed with these suggestions, and whether they would implement them. They almost always said yes, regardless of their true feelings and intentions, because other issues such as maintaining one's honor or one's face, maintaining smooth interpersonal relationships, avoiding disagreements and conflicts were more important than answering us honestly. As a result, we were misled and disappointed when the parents didn't follow through.

It took us a while to learn that among many Latinos, a

promise to do something or to comply with an expectation may not be meant literally. If a refusal would lead to an awkward or uncomfortable interpersonal moment or insult a person, especially someone in a position of authority, which was us, a promise may be little more than a way of maintaining smooth interpersonal relationships.

Socioeconomic class differences between the staff and students were no less important than ethnic and skin-color differences. The therapists, teachers, and volunteers from middle-class backgrounds had very different upbringings than the students. The middle-class staff were brought up to settle their differences peacefully without arguing. If an argument occurred, they were required to shake hands and make up. Definitely no fist fights. The students and the staff who grew up in poor neighborhoods tended to have another kind of upbringing. In our homes and neighborhoods, parents wouldn't lecture or punish us for arguing or fighting if the situation called for it. Some of our parents expected us to defend our honor with our fists if necessary, especially if someone said anything about our religion, female family members, et cetera. The middle-class staff tended to have been punished by their parents in non- physical ways such as by loss of material things, special privileges, being sent to their rooms, and so on. Those of us from the working class were used to being spanked or even hit with a strap.

As a result, the middle-class staff members tended to respond inappropriately to some of what occurred in the school and needed guidance from their poor relations. We poor folks had to explain to them that requiring students who were angry with each other to shake hands and "make friends" was a "no no" regardless of how right it seemed to them. We also had to insist that parents who used corporal punishment at home were not necessarily more abusive than their parents had been. (My mother had raised red welts on my backside with my own belt when she thought I needed it. And my sister had received the same treatment. No sexism there.)

One difference between the middle-class and working-class staff was especially tough to resolve, and I'm not sure that it was settled in all cases. Most of the boys carried knives with them for defensive purposes. This was the 60s, not the 90s— long before drive-by shootings, assault weapons, et cetera. Teenagers who carried weapons usually carried some sort of knife or linoleum cutter or, at worst, a zip gun, which was made from a car antenna and shot a single small-caliber bullet, very inaccurately, for a short distance.

The middle-class staff members wanted us to tell the boys not to carry knives and to make sure they didn't bring them to school. The two of us who had grown up in poor neighborhoods thought differently. We had learned that if two guys got involved in an argument, there was a greater chance that someone would get cut if only one of them had a knife than if they both had knives. Likewise, if someone with money but no knife was accosted by someone without money but with a knife, there was a good chance that the money would change hands. If they both had knives, however, the money was likely to stay right where it was. No wonder the boys felt safer carrying knives in their neighborhoods.

Knowing this, the two of us favored allowing the boys to bring knives to school as long as they didn't take them out. A therapist who understood the context of their lives agreed with us. We were three against the rest. The middle-class folks outnumbered us, but gave in reluctantly.

Yes, some of the boys did brandish their knives in the heat of an argument and lost them. However, since the offending knives were their property we paid them a fair price. Two of the students got the idea that they could make money by forcing us to buy their knives on a regular basis. We out-foxed them. We announced a new policy. We would continue to pay a dollar for the first knife, but only fifty cents for the second, a quarter for the third, and a dime for any additional ones. That put them out of business in a hurry.

Most educators are like I was when I started working with non- European Americans. They know very little about how their poor or non- European American students live. To correct this, personnel-preparation programs have to provide future teachers with first-hand experience with poor and non-European American students. As Ewing points out,

> Teacher-education programs must excel in preparing teachers and administrators who have an elevated level of authentic knowledge of African American culture; a deeper understanding of the impact African American culture has on behavior, learning styles, and preferred teaching styles; and a genuine appreciation for the valuable repertoire of experiences African American children bring to school . . . Preservice students must be immersed in extended, direct, real-life experiences in the African American milieu.(5)

In an ideal world, Ewing's recommendations would be followed by personnel-preparation programs that prepare educators to work with students from other ethnic backgrounds and students who are immigrants, migrants, homeless, and so on. However, in the less-than-ideal world in which we live, it would be impossible to provide them with the experiences they need in order to work effectively with all the different groups of diverse students in our schools. At the very least, however, teacher-preparation programs should target a few of those groups that are represented in their service areas and provide their students with intensive experience with these groups.

The staff divided along professional lines about issues as often as we did along socioeconomic lines. Let me give you two examples.

We seriously disagreed about the causes of conduct disorders and the best approaches to eliminate them. Most of the educators believed students with conduct disorders chose to act selfishly. They saw conduct disordered students as *unwilling* to respect the rights of others and thought that such students should be taught that there is a heavy cost to pay for behaving in an antisocial manner. The clinicians and one of the educators believed that conduct-disordered students only appeared to be unwilling to respect the rights of others. A combination of physiological characteristics and life experiences such as abuse, rejection, antisocial models, and the like caused them to be *unable* to behave in socially acceptable ways. We argued that if the teachers knew what caused students to seem to choose to take advantage of others, they would understand that their choice was actually shaped by factors and events beyond their control. We maintained that our job was to expose students with conduct disorders to experiences and model behavior that would correct or reshape the motivation that caused them to behave as they did, not to teach them a lesson. We never resolved the issue.

The clinicians and educators also disagreed about the role of what is now called social-skills training—teaching students the social skills they need to know in order to behave appropriately. (We used the concept, not the term.) Most of the educators thought that most of our emotionally disturbed students had not learned how to share, to wait their turn, to ask permission, to function cooperatively, to do their part of the work, to acknowledge their mistakes, to demonstrate their anger and resentment in acceptable ways, and so on. And they were eager to teach them how to behave differently. We clinicians and one of the teachers disagreed. From our point of view, most of the students knew how to behave appropriately. Their difficulty was that their emotional problems interfered with their ability to do so. Teaching social skills to the students who already knew them, but couldn't act on them was unnecessary. Social-skills training would be helpful for the one or two students whose emotional problems had prevented them from acquiring the skills they needed to relate positively to others. However, it wouldn't become useful until the emotional problems that had interfered with their acquisition of the skills were eliminated. This controversy was resolved within a few months.

Although ethnic, skin color, socioeconomic class, gender, and professional differences, like the ones I have just described, created some minor difficulties for us, the program was extremely successful. The director of the agency who had given me the job had intimated that we might have to return quite a few boys to the courts. In fact, during my three-year tenure, we only had to return one student. And I believe we could have succeeded with him if we hadn't grown so fast and taken in more students than the staff could handle effectively.

Everything was going great, and then the director of the agency retired. As I said at the beginning of the chapter, he was a visionary. Unfortunately, he was replaced by someone with a more traditional approach. The new director and the chief psychiatrist of the agency came to have a look at what we were doing. They read the students' records, observed the classes, and interviewed the teachers and therapists. A couple of weeks later, they said that they wanted me to return some of the students to the courts because they were too dangerous to be allowed to remain in the community. If they caused trouble in the community, the two of them explained, the agency and the program would be held responsible.

But they were all doing well, I protested. None of them had gotten into trouble, and they all had been in the program for at least a year, most for more than that. My protests had no affect. The agency still wanted me to return them. I refused. First they insisted, then they threatened, then they fired me and returned the students to the courts themselves. The students were all African Americans or Latinos. Not a European American among them.

I have often thought about what those kids must have felt when they were punished even though they had been behaving well, getting better, and overcoming their problems. I also thought a great deal about why the chief psychiatrist and the director of the agency treated them so unjustly. I came to the conclusion that neither of them came to the school to look for African American and Latino kids to ship back to court. I have no reason to believe that they hated African Americans or Latinos. What I believe happened was that they knew very little about non-European American kids. And, not understanding them, they were afraid of them. They said they were trying to protect society and the agency's good name, but they picked the wrong kids. There is no doubt in my mind, that if those kids had been European Americans, they would have had a better shake from society and its agents.

Judging from what research indicates about the virulence of prejudice and discrimination in education today, there is also little doubt in my mind that the same thing could easily happen today. I imagine that most regular educators, special educators, and psychologists believe that they are not biased against non-European American and poor students. But they are wrong! While some of them may not be biased, research indicates that most are, even if they are unaware of it. Let me cite a few examples.

Educators tend to use different classroom-management techniques with African American and European American students. In general, teachers spend more time on the lookout for possible misbehavior by African American students, especially males. When male students misbehave, educators are prone to criticize the behaviors of African American males and to use more severe punishments, including corporal punishment and suspension, with them. And when females misbehave, teachers treat African Americans more harshly than European Americans.

Teachers also relate to Latino students in a discriminatory manner. Although Latino students tend to prefer more positive reinforcement and feedback from their teachers than most European American students, teachers praise them less often and give them less positive feedback when they answer correctly or perform well. Teachers are also less likely to encourage them when they need encouragement, to accept their ideas, and to direct questions to them.

Poor students also receive unfair treatment in school. Beginning in primary school, teachers give them less attention and fewer rewards. Educators provide poor students, especially males, fewer social and instructional contacts, but more disciplinary and control contacts. And, when they discipline students, teachers in schools that serve predominantly poor students are more likely to endorse or use corporal punishments, verbal punishments, or suspension than teachers in schools attended by middle-class students.

When teachers evaluate the severity or deviancy of students' behavior problems, they judge the same transgressions as more severe or deviant when they are committed by African American male students than when they are committed by European American students. African American students who are seen as fun-loving, happy, cooperative, energetic and ambitious by African American teachers are viewed as talkative, lazy, fun-loving, high-strung, and frivolous by their European American teachers.

Teachers are more likely to refer poor and non-European American students than European American middle-class students for evaluation for possible placement in programs for students with emotional, and behavioral problems. When educators and psychologists evaluate these students, they tend to judge their work, performance, intellectual abilities, and social skills to be lower than objective data would indicate. When selecting the most appropriate placement for students with the same problems, they are more likely to choose a special-education program for non-European Americans and poor students and a regular-education program for middle- class European American students. And when they choose a special-education program for students, they are likely to recommend a more restrictive, custodial environment for non-European Americans and poor students than for middle-class European American students. Being poor and African American places students at even greater risk to be on the receiving end of teacher bias.

When I ask myself why educators treat students in such discriminatory ways, I find three major contributing factors. First, I believe that prejudice and discrimination toward people who are different than we are are pandemic diseases of human kind. Witness the tension, conflicts, and sometimes even outright wars caused by religious differences in Northern Ireland and India; by ethnic differences in Iraq, the former Yugoslavia, the Philippines, China, the former Soviet Union, Rwanda, and Burundi; by socioeconomic classes in Great Britain; by skin-color differences in South Africa, Australia, Great Britain, and Mexico; by language differences in Canada; and by whether individuals are immigrants or native-born citizens in Germany and other Western-European countries just to name a few. We seemed to be programmed to discriminate against people who do not belong to our group, or who look, talk, think, or act differently from us. Prejudice and discrimination are an ever-present danger against which we must constantly be vigilant.

Second, much of our prejudice is unconscious. Wanting to see ourselves in a good light, we hide our prejudice from ourselves. We usually don't notice that we call on one group of students more than another, expect more from one group than another, or reward and punish one group more than another. When we do realize what we are doing, we justify and rationalize our inappropriate behavior. We attribute to the students we discriminate against characteristics such as linguistic inadequacy, aggressiveness, cultural inferiority, and other stereotypes that pervade our society, thereby convincing ourselves that it's necessary to treat them the way we do. Being unaware of the discriminatory way we treat students and/or rationalizing it away, we have no need to change our behavior.

Unconscious prejudice is difficult to get a handle on. Here's an example from my past. Not too long after World War II ended, a large number of Puerto Rican Americans began moving into my neighborhood. The gang I hung out with and I had little, if anything, to do with the guys. However, one day my friend and I met two Puerto Rican girls who lived up the block. We talked under the stoop of one of the girls for a couple of hours and arranged to meet them after school the next day. When I came home from school the next day, my mother told me to forget my plans. When I asked what plans, she told me that one of the girl's mothers had asked her to keep me away from her daughter. I asked my mother why. Because I wasn't Puerto Rican, she explained. That puzzled me. I could understand that my mother might not want me to hang around with Puerto Rican girls (actually I knew that neither of my parents felt that way), but I couldn't believe that Puerto Rican parents would not want their daughters to hang out with me. If, at that moment, someone had told me that meant I was prejudiced, I would have laughed in his or her face. How could I be prejudiced, I would have argued. I liked a Puerto Rican girl.

Third, as I stated above, many educators discriminate against students who are unlike them because they fear them.

In 1967, I had been fired from one job, the Phoenix School, but I still had my teaching job at a local university, where I was in my second year of directing a training program for teachers of emotionally disturbed students. The last day of that school year I received a lesson I would never forget. It occurred in a local eating-and-drinking establishment where I was spending the evening with the students who had taken the final exam in a course I had taught.

Around 10:30, I noticed that the only students remaining were six or seven female fellowship students. They were looking at me funny. They told me that I had given a lot to them and now they were going to give me something. It didn't sound like a present. They proceeded to tell me that I had been treating female students unfairly. I gave the impression that I was a caring, concerned professor who would be available to the students on both a professional and personal level. I had lived up to that promise with the male students. However, I had kept the female students at arms length, seeming to be afraid of any kind of closeness with them. What was I going to do, they asked, ignore half the world's population? Until that moment I had not realized that I treated male and female students differently. The realization shocked me, but made sense. I had been perfectly content to attend an all-boys high school and a male college and to run an all-male treatment school. With the particular moral upbringing I had received, I could understand that I felt safer keeping my distance from women, especially if they showed any interest in me, even as a professor.

I resolved never to do that again. That evening was my first step toward looking at the gender issues in my life and in education.

A few days later I carried the school flag at graduation. I wasn't sure why I had been chosen for the honor, but I thought I knew. I had arranged to transfer the local school district's program for seven-to-nine-year-old students with severe emotional problems from their cramped facility in the district to the expensive state-of-the-art demonstration facilities in the School of Education building. The facility had been vacant and unused for two years, a fact that had been a source of embarrassment for the School of Education. How could I have foreseen that the act that earned me the gratitude of my chair and dean would also end my stay at the university?

Only one day into the following academic year, I went from someone who could do no wrong at the university to someone who could do no right. Here's how it happened. Although well over 90 percent of the students who attended the local school district were European Americans, well over 90 percent of the students in their special education program were African Americans. So naturally the staff and I tried to adapt the school milieu, curriculum, instructional and classroom-management approaches, and so on to the cultural realities of both the European American and African American students.

It only took a few hours for the departmental chair, who considered himself to be a liberal person, to order me to change everything back to look and sound like what European American professors tend to be comfortable with. No soul music! Classical and other forms of quiet music only. No loud, emotional talking or shouting! Students are to act like ladies and gentlemen. No getting out of chairs! Students are to sit quietly and motionless in their seats like good children. No anything African American.

I tried to explain to him what we were doing and why, without success. Within the week, the chair had relieved me of my responsibilities in the school. Although he had no experience working with emotionally disturbed children, he appointed himself director.

The situation soon heated up. Without my knowledge, the African American graduate students and graduates of the program, with the participation of some of European American students, started a letter-writing campaign to reverse the chair's decision. He, in turn, wrote an extremely derogatory letter about me to the dean (which I was never allowed to read). The upshot was that the dean asked both of us to volunteer to leave. We both complied– I at the end of the school year, he sometime later.

That was the second job I had lost since I started working with students of color. I lost a third job, a part-time one, the following year, but I kept another part-time job.

Perhaps I should discuss these two jobs briefly. The job I lost was as a consultant to the adolescent unit in a state mental hospital. Having learned a lot during the preceding eleven years, I had been doing some of my best work there for approximately two years. Then an incident occurred. Naturally, it had to do with skin-color issues. One of the students, a twenty-two-year-old disturbed European-American female, who also tested at the developmentally disabled level on an I.Q. test, primarily because she had been institutionalized for perhaps fifteen years, was caught having sex in the basement with an African American male. Claiming that the female student was not smart enough to resist the invitation of the male student and was therefore intellectually incapable of managing her sex life, the administration decided to sterilize her without her consent. The male student was also punished, but not sterilized. The teachers protested the decision to the administration and called it racist because similar incidents that did not involve white females and black males had been handled differently. The administration got back at them by firing me. Eventually the teachers contacted the news media and local and state officials. It was a mess. Things got better, but too late for the student who had been declared incompetent and was sterilized.

The job I kept was in a drug rehabilitation center set up as an alternative to prison for adolescents and young adult drug abusers between the ages of 16 thru 21 who had committed crimes. I had two responsibilities. One of my responsibilities was to help the teachers and principal, who had no experience with adolescents and young adults who abused drugs, or with students with emotional and behavioral problems, to adapt their approaches to their students' needs. The other was to assist the counselors, who were mature adult ex-drug abusers themselves, to adapt their techniques to the teenagers and young adults in the program.

Although the educational consultation quickly bore fruit, I made only very slow progress with the counselors during the first year, mainly because we were from different worlds. They had all graduated from adult drug rehabilitation programs that had included heavy doses of punishment, shame, ridicule, and confrontation for misdeeds and rewards both personal and material for improved behavior. Since they had succeeded in their adult programs, they believed that a similar approach would work for teenagers. The only inroad I made with them was that they made me the therapist of a few students who were fighting their approach.

Then one day they asked to meet with me. They said they had learned that the students I was working with were much more open with me than they had been with them and asked me to teach them some counseling techniques. I asked them what kinds of things they wanted the students to be open about. They answered that they wanted students to admit when they broke the rules in the rehabilitation center (stole things, got into fights, got high, et cetera), to tell them when they hung around with drug abusers in their neighborhoods during day trips or overnights, and to advise them when they were afraid that they might slip and use drugs if they went on trips to their communities.

What would happen to the students if they admitted that they broke the rules in the center or in the community? They would be punished. They might lose some privileges, get their hair shaved off, have to wear a stocking cap, or a billboard, go down a level, and so forth. And how would the counselors react if students admitted they were worried that they might lose their self control and succumb to the temptation to abuse drugs if they were allowed to spend unsupervised time in the community? They wouldn't let them go. Then why should students be honest with their counselors, I asked, if they are going to be punished or denied unsupervised time in the community?

What would I do, they asked. If they stole something they might have to make amends, I answered. If they got high they might have to get rid of the offending drug and explain how they got it in the center. If they were afraid they might abuse drugs if they were unsupervised in the community they might be encouraged to assess their ability to resist the temptation and then decide whether they should go. However, I wouldn't punish them for being honest or for asking for help. I definitely would not shave off their hair or make them wear a stocking cap, or a billboard. The counselors couldn't have it both ways. They couldn't punish students for volunteering information and asking for help and then expect them to do so.

That meeting changed my relationship with the counselors. Within a short period of time, they began to counsel students rather than mete out rewards and punishments. They certainly did not change their approach 100 percent. However, they did react differently to students who voluntarily discussed their behavior during counseling sessions and to those they caught misbehaving.

I have had similar experiences consulting with many teachers and administrators who rely inordinately on level systems and/or positive and negative reinforcements. In general, these administrators and teachers believe that their students are willful and choose to misbehave, and therefore need to learn the consequences of their actions. What about the students who cannot control themselves because they are assaulted by intense emotions, or because they are motivated by irrational or defensive thought processes, I ask.

Teachers and administrators in correctional facilities that rely too much on consequences typically say those kinds of kids are sent to other programs, not correctional facilities. Teachers and administrators in special education programs who over-use rewards and punishments justify their actions by claiming that they take that into consideration. However, they seem to be unable to explain how.

A number of years ago, I was hired to be one of a number of professors who taught special education courses to a group of teachers in the California State Correctional Program. Most of the teachers I observed were doing a terrible job. They weren't terrible people, but except for two or three of them, they were definitely terrible teachers. (If they had been terrible people they wouldn't have volunteered for the additional work they had to do in order to obtain their special education credentials.) A typical class looked like this. Twelve to twenty students sat at desks writing on worksheets while their teacher looked down, attending to paper work. Occasionally, if the teacher heard a noise or noticed a hand waving he or she would look up.

When a student finished a worksheet he raised his hand and was invited to the teacher's desk where he would turn in his completed sheet. The teacher would place a mark next to his name giving him credit for one sheet and allow the student to remove the next sheet from his folder. At the end of each period the teacher would rate each student on the basis of the number of sheets he completed and his compliant behavior. At the end of the week the ratings of all the teachers would be tallied. If the student didn't lose more than a specified number of rating points, he kept all of his privileges or was given additional ones. If he had been marked down too often, he lost privileges such as getting things from the facility store, attending recreational events, participating in off-grounds trips, and visiting off grounds. If his behavior was really bad, he was punished in addition to losing privileges.

With that much power and control over their students, the teachers were able to require their students to do the most ridiculous work, and most of their students complied. Most students were prepared to complete any number and any kind of trivial, irrelevant, boring, nonsensical worksheets to avoid losing their privileges. Those who were too emotionally disturbed or rebellious to do so suffered the consequences. The less disturbed or rebellious lost privileges. The ones with the most serious problems were punished severely.

I met with the school administration a number of times in a vain attempt to get them to modify their punitive approach. They could see what I was driving at, they responded. But they were only one division of the facility. It operated on the point system and they couldn't change it.

There was something I could do. All of my students had to complete a practicum course during their final semester. To assist their staff to complete their practica, the administrators identified a group of inmates/students who needed special education and allowed the teachers-in-training to spend part of their day teaching them. I informed the teachers that they could do whatever they wanted to or had to do in their regular classes. However, during their special education classes they could not use the point system.

Teaching without the awesome power of the institution behind them made them extremely insecure. Having to rely only on the special education techniques they had learned made them exceedingly anxious. However, in the end, all but one of them rose to the challenge. When their practica were over, they had learned how to succeed without relying on their power and thanked me for it.

I hoped that the special education teachers we had trained would have a positive influence on their many colleagues. Unfortunately, that didn't happen. The program remained the same, at least during the few years I kept up with it. However, quite a few of the teachers we trained decided that they could not continue to be a part of the system they had once fit into so easily and found other jobs. That was good for them, but awful for the students they left behind to suffer through the old ways.

Back to being asked to resign my position at the university. Luckily, I was still in demand. In a matter of days, I received an offer to join the faculty of the Department of Psychiatry of Albert Einstein Medical School. They had a huge community mental health program going in the southeast Bronx and needed people who had experience with African Americans and Latinos. My job description was to set up a children's and adolescents' mental health center and train a group of community people to help staff it. Since I had joined the faculty precipitously, I had to wait for the administration to obtain the necessary funding.

While waiting for my permanent assignment to begin, I was asked to start a mental health clinic in a school for pregnant teenagers. The school "served" 50 students who had been pushed out of their regular schools and uprooted from the programs they had been attending and the friends and teachers who might have supported them. Evidently, the New York City Board of Education assumed that either pregnancy was a contagious disease or teenagers who saw pregnant girls in class would want to be just like them.

The school was grossly inadequate. It had only enough classrooms for four academic subjects, no laboratories, art, music, vocational training, special education, remedial education, recreational facilities, lunchroom, library, school yard, or windows to the outside. No anything else—just four small academic classrooms and a few offices.

A small percentage of the 50 girls who were emotional disturbed could have used a special education program. Many were dealing with serious situational emotional problems. Quite a few of them were coping really well with their situation. Most of the students needed the assistance of a good social worker. Fifteen to 20 percent of them could have benefited from good psychological services. That was to be my job. Five African American female educators, a Latina female social worker and fifty 13-to-18 year-old pregnant African American and Latino students were presented with a white male professor of psychiatry who had time to kill until his assignment started. I was told later that I was not a welcome sight. They would have preferred someone of color or at least a female.

At first the school seemed surrealistic. The teachers were following the prescribed curriculum to a T. They did not mention, much less talk to, the students about their problems at home, their need to make major decisions such as whether to keep their babies, what to do about the babies' fathers, should they and how could they continue their education after their babies were born, and so on. They were teachers and they were supposed to teach. They did not accommodate their approaches or schedules to the students' morning sickness, fatigue, depression, anxiety, and so on. The mothers-to-be were supposed to act happy, attentive, and interested. The teachers' actions said, "Please girls, put on a happy face." Most tried; few could manage it. Cheerful teachers in front of sad, depressed, frightened kids.

My assignment was to set up a counseling program. However, I also saw my job as helping the teachers realize that they could be more effective if they adapted their approaches to the students' situational and emotional problems; helping them see that they could play a productive role in advising students; and breaking down artificial barriers to communication between the teaching staff and students.

I thought these three goals would take months to achieve. However, once again I was naive. In less than a month the school was completely turned around. The teachers weren't males and they weren't European Americans. They were African American women who understood what the students were up against. All it took was permission and perhaps a little encouragement from an authority figure to free them to do what they knew in their hearts was the right thing.

Counseling the girls proved to be the greater challenge for me since I had never worked with African American or Latina females. Luckily, the very knowledgeable Puerto Rican social worker who I was supposed to supervise took me under her wing.

Although the staff at the school were in the students' corner, many of them had to deal with other prejudiced people who were not. I would like to describe an incident that illustrates the kind of prejudice that affected their lives and continues to influence the lives of African American and Latino students like them. One of the students who I was counseling, a 15-year-old dark-skinned Puerto Rican American, Lucila, asked me if I could also help her 17-year-old sister, Josephina. Josephina was shoplifting and stealing tips customers had left for the waiters and waitresses in restaurants. Lucila had gone along with her a few times. They had two close calls and wanted to stop. They would, they both assured me, if they could get the money they needed another way.

They lived with their mother, an, alcoholic, who survived on welfare. Lucila had attended classes irregularly during the previous year until she transferred to our special school. She had sixth-grade reading skills and fifth-grade math skills. She seldom did any homework or even came to class prepared, claiming that she was too tired to concentrate on school work. That might have been true, except for the fact that had been her pattern long before she had become pregnant. She said that she had stopped her occasional use of marijuana and various pills (she had never used cocaine or heroine) when she learned in our school that drugs could harm her baby.

Josephina was in her senior year. She had done moderately well in school. However, she had begun to skip school regularly a couple of months before I met her. She told me that although she had hoped to graduate and attend college, she had given up on the idea because she could not imagine how she would be able to support her sister and herself and go to school at the same time. Josephina denied using any drugs, except marijuana, and then only occasionally.

I didn't think they were "running a number" on me. Thinking that Josephina, at least, might change her behavior once she could afford to do so, I met with the family caseworker in the welfare department and asked if the department could provide them with the small amount of additional money they claimed they needed to stop stealing and tread the straight-and-narrow path. Their caseworker, a European American woman turned me down. "You don't know these people," she told me. "They'll waste the money on drugs. The only work people like them can do is cleaning houses and taking care of kids."

I couldn't let her get away with that. A few days later I met with her supervisor. This time, instead of introducing myself as a psychologist at the school, I made sure to mention that I was *Doctor* Grossman and a faculty member of the Department of Psychiatry of Albert Einstein Medical School. I also said that the case worker was prejudiced and alluded to the fact that I had been thinking of saying so to the appropriate authorities. The result of the meeting was that the supervisor agreed to increase the family's benefits and to provide financial support to Josephina through a vocational rehabilitation program if she became a full-time college student.

The last time I saw Josephina, shortly before I left New York for points south, she was attending The City University of New York. But what would have happened to her if no one had advocated for her, or if I wasn't on the faculty at Albert Einstein, or hadn't threatened to take the issue to the authorities?

Lucila's story, unfortunately, did not have a happy ending. She had serious emotional and learning problems and had little faith in herself. She needed a lot more than she was getting at the school. I left the school to start my permanent assignment, setting up a childrens' and adolescents' treatment center, a few months before she had her baby. Without sustained counseling she went downhill.

The last time I checked up on her, she was being supported by welfare. She had strung herself out on heroin almost immediately after her baby was born and was spending the little money she had for drugs, instead of food. The last thing I did for her was to accompany her to a child-protection program.

I finished training the treatment center staff right on schedule and told the administration that we were ready to go to work. Unfortunately, they weren't ready to put us to work and never were. Eventually I realized that the white professionals who ran the program had very little faith in the people they were supposed to be helping or training. Instead of psychotherapy, they were pushing pills. Instead of drug-rehabilitation programs, they offered methadone. I was totally disillusioned and beginning to think that most, but certainly not all, white professionals were not very concerned about the welfare of people of color. It appeared to me that for most white people, the helping professions – teaching, psychology, psychiatry and so on – were lucrative gigs and little more. It was time to leave another job.

My experiences with prejudice and discrimination where I worked, the rebellions going on in some of America's major cities, and the violent reactions to the non-violent civil rights movement in the South all led me to think that there was a kind of war going on. People were taking sides, and I found myself on the other side. I found my ideas were much better accepted by African Americans and Latinos than European Americans. And my African American and Latino colleagues didn't want to fire me. I also realized that I was more comfortable with the African Americans and Latinos I had been working with, even the extremely militant ones, than the European Americans. I have to admit that I was becoming prejudiced against white people.

Exciting things were going on in the South. I decided to join the faculty of an historically black college. Tuskegee was the most famous of all the black colleges and it was about as deep South as you could go. So I resigned my position at the medical school and took a job there.

I thought my ideas would be better received and I would enjoy life more in a black college in a black town. But I had also been told something while I was attending a conference that made me just a little unsure about that.

I was having breakfast with two African American professors, hoping to get their feedback about my decision to leave New York for Tuskegee. I figured they would level with me since we had been friends for a number of years. One professor ducked my questions by saying that it had been many years since he had been in the South. The other professor angrily told me off. "We can help our own people", he declared. "We don't need you. If you really want to help black people, change your own people. They need you more than we do."

My friend kept his attitude towards me for few years; then it disappeared.

Thinking back to the incident, I can now see that his attitude was no less racist and prejudiced than those of the many people I had locked horns with during the previous four years. He had stopped seeing me, the individual person, and saw me, the white man. I too was prejudiced. I rejected white people's prejudice towards people of color, but I accepted his prejudice toward white people and me. An African American friend once said this to me.

> The white man can afford not to be prejudiced. He can give the black man the benefit of the doubt until he gets to know who the black man really is because the white man has all the power in this country. As powerless as the black man is in this country, he can't afford to trust the white man. He's better off being suspicious and on guard until he knows if the white man is an exception to the rule. And there are so few exceptions, it's not worth the time it takes to get to know him anyway, just to be disappointed one more time.

Chapter 3

TUSKEGEE, ALABAMA

I ARRIVED IN TUSKEGEE in 1969. The campus was beautiful: ivy-cloaked buildings sitting on little knolls and nestling in small glens, shade trees, and a profusion of summer flowers lining footpaths that wound through the lawn to connect the buildings. The facilities and equipment, however, were nothing like what I had seen at predominately white universities.

(Today, the infrastructure at historically black colleges and universities is much improved, but it is still way behind predominately white universities because of the years of discriminatory funding practices. It's still a poor-kid, rich-kid story.)

Although separate but equal had been declared unconstitutional and many changes had occurred in the town, whites and blacks still led separate lives. The local whites had left the public school system, but they left a European American superintendent in charge of the schools they fled. And they moved much of the expensive equipment to their private schools.

The local movie house had been closed by its European American owner because the African Americans in town refused to sit in the balcony. The local restaurants were integrated, but the European-American-owned establishments that had tables and chairs had been turned into take-out places. African Americans had been given jobs in the local banks and shops, but only after a boycott and only as tellers and clerks. Hardly any African Americans were running cash registers in European American owned stores. An African American entrepreneur had built a supermarket to compete with the white-owned establishments, but it had mysteriously burned. African Americans had recently *earned* the right to use public toilets in the local gas stations. However, that had not happened until a young black male, Sammy Young, had been shot to death while trying to use a "for-whites-only" toilet, and the person who shot him had been exonerated by an all-European-American jury.

I taught abnormal and adolescent psychology during my first summer at Tuskegee. I was very excited the morning of my first class. Once again I thought I was prepared. I was confident that I was less naive about the African American students I would be teaching and the students I would be preparing them to teach than I had been when I started the Phoenix School in 1965. After all, I had taught severely emotionally disturbed students. I had been on the faculty of four universities. I had already directed a teacher-training program. I had been working with African Americans for five years and so on. It turned out that once again I was more naive than I realized, especially about the reception I was about to receive from the students and townspeople.

I got to class early Thursday morning. It was only 7:45, but the room was already hot because neither of the air conditioners in the windows worked. I wrote my name, office hours, and telephone number on the blackboard and waited for the students.

At 8:10, there were only two students in the room; so I waited some more. At 8:15 I started with only 11 of the 19 students on my class list. (Different groups of people have disparate concepts of punctuality.)

I began the class by telling them about the course.

"Abnormal psychology is supposed to explain abnormal people or abnormal behavior. Abnormal means more than different; it usually means something bad, or at least undesirable. But I've spent my career working with so-called abnormal people like delinquents, emotionally dist. . ."

"Oh! Are we abnormal too? That why you came here to teach us?" someone called out.

The students were all staring at me and I could sense their let's-see-how-whitey-handles-that-one attitudes. My mind went blank for a second; then I recovered.

"No," I answered. "Working with people in trouble and training students to help people are two different things to me. I came here to teach college students, not to work with abnormal people." Then I asked the students where they could find a lot of abnormal people in one place?"

"Right here,"

The class laughed. I looked toward the back and saw a student enjoying the laughter his wise crack had caused.

I figured he meant me, but I pretended I didn't and continued the class, writing the students' answers on the board: here, jails, state hospitals, et cetera. Then I began to cite statistics that indicated that African Americans were over represented in each category.

"That's a lie," someone interrupted.

"Go, head on man," another called out.

"That's because white folks takes care of their own kind," a third insisted, raising his voice above the racket being made by the students talking to each other.

I noticed a student sitting quietly with his hand raised. I pointed to him. He rose slowly, waiting until he had everyone's attention. "You ever read *How To Lie With Statistics,*" he asked, fixing me with an intense stare.

"Yeah," I answered. "Why? Are you trying to say the statistics I read are a lie?"

"Yeah it's a lie. White folks be putting out anything they want. They're always doing studies on us." The class smiled. "Ya'll come down here to write books. Stay just long enough to get your research done. Then you're gone."

I knew he meant me. But I didn't want to react to the challenge.

The class was buzzing, but I continued to read some more statistics about prisons and mental hospitals. Students continued to shout out angry objections to the statistics, but I kept reading until the class ended.

The next morning I discovered a riddle that someone had written on the blackboard. "What's the only difference between a honkey and a bucket of shit? The bucket."

(As the research indicates, African American students are definitely more outspoken and direct than European Americans. I was challenged more times by students my first few weeks in Tuskegee than during the preceding six years teaching predominately white students at four universities. White students might think something about you, but at least in situations in which they were the majority, black students would tell you.)

During my first class in adolescent psychology, I asked the students from rural areas to write a few sentences about what they thought life was like for black teenagers growing up in urban areas and the students from urban areas to do the same for rural teenagers. I compiled and duplicated what each group had written. The next day I asked the two groups of students to sit on opposite sides of the room facing each other and gave them copies of what the other group had written without saying a single word. Some of their ideas about teenagers' sex lives, drugs, and so on were very outrageous, especially for those days.

At first a few murmurs rose from each side, then a few comments, denials, protests, recriminations, shouts, screams. The students were really going at each other. And I still hadn't said anything. Suddenly the dean and the assistant dean burst into the room. People had heard the commotion, assumed that the students were angry at me, and notified the administrators who had rushed over to rescue me. False alarm.

(As the author I quoted in the previous section stated,

> "Whites want social interaction to operate at an emotion-
> ally subdued level. To realize this goal they first establish
> the rule that expressive behavior shall be subdued, which
> develops sensibilities capable of tolerating only relatively
> subdued outputs . . . . Black cultural norms desire levels of
> public interaction that are more emotionally intense.
> Consequently they allow individuals to express themselves
> at the level at which feelings are felt.")

When I started teaching, I wasn't sure what the students were learning from my lectures because very few of them took notes. And I was put off by the fact that most of the women kept busy cooling themselves off with their Martin Luther King fans. I wondered whether they didn't care or have interest in what was going on or had different ways of functioning in class. Later I found that the students behaved that way in all of their classes.

While in New York, I had started giving students the option of taking oral or written exams. Oral exams have advantages, but my white students almost always chose writ-ten exams. Tuskegee students were different; the vast major-ity preferred oral exams. (As research indicates African American students tend to be aural/oral learners.)

Although it took time to get a proposal funded by the fed-eral government, the university received the funds it needed to support a training program for teachers of emotionally dis-turbed and behavior- disordered students. I directed the pro-gram and also taught some of the required courses. The training program for teachers of students with emotional problems started with maybe 14 or so full time graduate stu-dents, most of whom were receiving fellowships. Wanting to set a tone of informality, I scheduled a full day of class at my apartment for the first day. At first we sat around discussing the program, getting to know each other, et cetera. Then I introduced the first topic on my agenda, making curriculum relevant to African Americans. After we had all agreed that relevancy was an important goal, I asked, "Your friend the policeman, in or out?" Seeing a puzzled look on most of the students' faces, I reminded them of the stories that appeared in many curricula for young children about your friend the policeman, your friend the fireman, your friend the baker, and so on. And I asked, "Should your friend the policeman be included or eliminated?"

The rebellions (or riots if you have a different point of view) in Watts, Detroit, and other cities, during which people pelted police officers and fire fighters with stones and shot at them, were still fresh in the students' minds, as were reports about and often personal experiences with police brutality and misconduct toward African Americans. I didn't have to do or say another thing. The students were off and running. They spent the whole morning discussing that one question until I announced I was about to serve lunch. They never got off the topic and never reached any kind of consensus. From one side I heard: Who are you to decide who is and isn't someone's enemy? You're not their parents. Children aren't old enough to be told things like that; they're too immature. They don't know how to handle that kind of information. Don't you have any experience with children? Tell them things like that, and some might get their heads handed to them. That's like giving our warriors spears and sending them out to fight folks with automatic weapons. How can you tell children not to read a story in their readers?

Others countered with statements such as: We have to tell our children as early as possible who their enemies are. If we don't tell them the truth they'll find out soon enough, and then it will be too late. It's better to fight with spears then to not fight at all. Rosa Parks didn't have automatic weapons;

she didn't even have a spear.

A few students, who were for a compromise, made comments like: We don't have to say anything for or against policemen. We can just take the story out and let the parents tell their children what they want.

With exceptions, most of the students who were against telling children that policemen were not always their friends were female and/or middle class. Most of those who wanted to tell children the truth about policemen, as they they believed it to be, were males and/or from poor backgrounds.

(What a lesson in diversity. I can't imagine how anyone, no matter how prejudiced, could continue to stereotype African Americans into one group, believe that one black person could tell white people what black people think, et cetera, after listening to that conversation. It would have to be impossible. I hope.)

Although the graduate students were unable to agree about this particular controversial issue, they did agree about many other changes they would institute in order to make the curriculum relevant to black children and youth. You would think that by now, 30 years later, educators would almost reflexively try to make their curricula relevant to all of the students in their programs. Research and my personal experience, however, indicate that is still an elusive goal.

I want to talk about two other examples of the diversity among the African American students. They are examples of the identity problems students of color experience growing up in this white-dominated society, when they are under pressure by opposing values and beliefs. They occurred while I was counseling students.

The informal counseling program I did at Tuskegee started as a result of two students' whose grades were below the minimum acceptable level to remain in school, asking me to intervene with the administration on their behalf. I offered to work with the students if they were allowed to continue their studies. The administration added to the list two more students who had also flunked. As a result, the four students were allowed to continue in school provided that they met with me for help with problems that caused them to do so poorly. Because the problems that had contributed to their failures weren't academic, I soon found myself counseling them about personal issues. After a while the word got out that students could talk to me unofficially and that I didn't have to report to university.

In the first example, a student asked me to help him resolve a problem he was having because he belonged to the ROTC unit on campus. His girlfriend and two best friends, who were part of a student anti-war movement trying to close ROTC, were threatening to disassociate themselves from him unless he quit. He agreed with them that the Vietnam War was a "white man's" war. He didn't want to risk his life for white people. And he didn't want to lose his girlfriend or his best friends. On the other hand, without the ROTC money he would have to drop out of school. And he would have to let down his parents who had made great sacrifices to send him to college and were counting on him to provide the financial help his brothers and sisters would need to follow in his footsteps.

Two seniors, both of whom had huge Afro's and wore the dashikis and other African adornments that were extremely popular at the time, came to me separately about the same problem. They were about to commence job hunting. Some of their friends planned to cut their hair and dress in suits in order to please potential employers. Others intended to show up looking like "black was beautiful" and take their chances. The two students in question wanted to join the second group, but they were concerned about the possible consequences.

Middle-class European American teachers who are comfortable with the dominant culture tend to be oblivious of the many identity conflicts students of color, even quite young ones, experience when their teachers insist that they immediately adapt to the schools' European American middleclass culture. People's guesstimates about how many of these students think of their conflicts in terms like "acting white" or "talking white" vary considerably. However, whether the students think in such terms or not, many of them are troubled by cultural-identity conflicts about behaving in the ways preferred by their middle-class white teachers.

Getting back to the students in the training program, I wanted my students to see some of the programs for emotionally disturbed and behavior disordered students in the area. Although there had been a big increase in classes for students with developmental disabilities and emotional and behavioral problems throughout the South following integration of the schools (black students were grossly over represented in the programs), there were no programs for students with emotional and behavioral problems in our immediate vicinity. I settled for the nearby program for delinquent kids.

The contrast between the program I had taught in in New York and the program in Alabama was even more shocking than I had anticipated.

The black counselor they assigned to be our guide wanted to give us an overview of the program while the "wards" were eating. I thought the students would learn more by visiting the dining room and dormitories. So we started our tour in the living quarters. I asked the guide about the lack of sheets and pillowcases— which he said were too expensive, the lack of chests of drawers and closets—which he said weren't necessary because the wards weren't allowed personal belongings, and the lack of doors on the toilet stalls— which he said were against institutional policy. Then I encouraged the students to try out the beds which sank into hammock-like shapes under their weight.

I asked the counselor if he knew what percent of the wards

were placed for delinquency rather than PINS petitions. What were PINS petitions, a student asked. I explained that in some states the courts distinguished between teenagers who committed acts such as burglary, assault, and rape, which were adult crimes, and teenagers who had just committed acts such as truancy from school, running away from home, and refusing to obey parents, which weren't crimes, but indicated that they were persons in need of supervision by the court–or PINS.

"You mean some of these boys aren't delinquents?" a female student asked.

I directed her question to the guide who explained that many of the wards were PINS's.

"But they're all treated the same in terms of the rules and regulations?"

The counselor agreed reluctantly.

In the dining hall, in answer to a question, the counselor explained that the potbelly stove in the middle of the room provided heat in winter.

"That little stove does the whole thing?" a student asked.

Again the counselor nodded his agreement begrudgingly.

Then we asked about the absence of forks and knives in the silverware trays. The counselor, becoming more and more defensive, said the wards ate everything with soup spoons because knives and forks could be made into weapons. Even the soup spoons had to be counted, or they would be stolen and turned into weapons. By the time the students were given a tour of the school, they began to ask the questions.

"How come ya'll classes are segregated, brother?"

"They're not."

"There are no white boys in this reading class and there weren't any blacks in the other one."

"We group them according to reading levels. They stay with their groups for all their classes."

The students moaned. That must have been the straw that broke the camel's back because the counselor stopped defending the institution.

"No sisters, either," he added. "Before integration the black brothers and sisters were all here and the white boys and girls were up north near Birmingham. When they integrated the races, white folks made sure the black brothers were nowhere near the white girls. Now they're still segregating only this time it's by sexes."

I asked about their special education program. There wasn't any; that was par for the course in correctional facilities in New York as well.

At the end of the tour, I asked the counselor about the effectiveness of the program.

"What percentage of the boys make it?"

"Where to?" he replied sarcastically. "Most of them will be back here within a year after they leave if they don't graduate to prison first. Nobody's going to give these brothers a break. No jobs for black folks as it is. Sure ain't going to be any for our graduates."

(It seems that times haven't changed that much. Discrimination in employment is still a problem. We still track African Americans in school and they are still over represented in correctional facilities and special education programs for students with emotional and behavioral problems.)

Let me tell you a little bit more about segregation in Alabama state institutions at the time. Alabama was beginning to deinstitutionalize developmentally disabled individuals who had been warehoused in their state institutions to halfway houses as a result of a suit against the state commissioner of mental health. (Actually he had purposefully instigated the suit against himself for the clients' benefit.) The commissioner asked me to represent him in efforts to develop halfway houses for the people who could not be returned to their communities, either because they were not ready or because they had no families who would accept them.

The mental health officials in various communities were very concerned about integration issues. At that time, few of them could accept the possibility that developmentally disabled blacks and whites would have to live in the same halfway house. Part of my job was to help them work through their reservations. My comments and suggestions pretty much fell on deaf ears. Perhaps they weren't ready for what I had to say. Perhaps they needed to hear it from one of their own. Perhaps my solutions were too naive. Perhaps I didn't know how to present them in a more palatable way. Or perhaps I was too prejudiced against white people to be able to work cooperatively with them. Whatever the reason, I wasn't disappointed when an unforeseen circumstance relieved me of my responsibilities.

(The unforeseen circumstance was the firing of the commissioner. Maybe it shouldn't have been unforeseen. Maybe I should have realized that, at that time, any commissioner of mental health in Alabama who had chosen me to represent him must have already placed his position in jeopardy.)

Visiting programs and schools in Alabama drove home the great disparity that "separate but equal" had created in the South. I had observed the discrepancies between the schools, hospitals, and other facilities for whites and blacks when I worked in the southeast Bronx, Harlem, and Bedford-Stuyvesant. However the results of unequal financing really hit home when I moved to the South. Not that long after I arrived at Tuskegee, I was driving to Montgomery with a friend, asking questions along the way. Approaching a school, I asked if it was a black or white school. My friend's expression turned angry. "Look at that school yard—no grass, no asphalt, almost no equipment. How many schools do you have to see before you can tell our raggedy schools from theirs?"

During those days, the federal government was attempting to redress these inequities at the both the public school and university level, but in a strange way. Let me explain. One day, on a bulletin board at Columbia University, I saw a flyer announcing the availability of "minority" scholarships for black student in various graduate programs in education. Because I received my doctorate from Columbia, I was well aware of the difference between the facilities and financial support I enjoyed as a graduate student at Columbia and the conditions under which my students at Tuskegee studied. So I knew which university really needed the funds.

I already knew the kinds of biased and irrelevant education and psychology programs Columbia provided non-European American graduate students. Having taken over 90 credits of graduate courses there, I also knew how biased the professors' instructional and assessment techniques were for non-European American students. I was convinced that despite Columbia's excellent and well-deserved reputation for academic excellence, African Americans would probably learn more of what they needed to know and feel more comfortable attending a primarily black university. Anger and outrage swelled up in me. How dare the government decide that African Americans should go to Columbia, I muttered to myself as I controlled my impulse to tear the flyer from the wall.

Recently, while watching "Sixty Minutes", I learned of a more-current approach to solving skin color educational inequities that evoked a similar reaction in me. (1) It seems that in 1994, the court decided to provide millions of dollars over a ten-year period for scholarships to encourage white students to enroll at Alabama State University, a historically black university. The court somehow believed that was a good idea to encourage white students who had no interest in attending a black college other than having their expenses paid to attend Alabama State. Better to use the money to redress the under funding that Alabama State and other historically black schools had endured for so many years and let any white students who want to attend the school compete with the other students for financial assistance. By the way, to add insult to injury, during the first four years of the program, African Americans needed a B average to qualify for financial aid; white students needed only a C average.

During the years that I taught at Tuskegee University, unless I went to a bank or a store, I was the only white person. At the beginning, I felt self-conscious and awkward. However, after a while, I forgot that I was white. That's the truth. I forgot that I was white until something brought it to my attention. Usually it was a racial incident provoked by some prejudiced black or white person who didn't like where I was or who I was associating with. Every once in a while, a white person would show up unexpectedly somewhere where "he or she had no business being." Typically, that happened when I was having a good time with my friends in a local black club or playing in a black band in a club somewhere in Alabama or Georgia. I would notice the strange white face and suddenly realize that I, too, was white. That would upset me because I hated the feeling of being different. It got so that any time I saw a white face where it didn't belong I got so angry I felt like telling the person to leave and go back to where white people belonged. I got to hate the sight of white people. Bizarre, wasn't it? So in 1973, when it was time for me to move on, returning to the white world was not something I was looking forward to.

Chapter 4

FT. LAUDERDALE, BOSTON, AND HAWAII

THE WHITE WORLD I REENTERED was strange at first, but it quickly became familiar. My first stop was a year on the beach in Ft. Lauderdale. Then followed a post doctoral fellowship at the Tufts New England Medical Center, during which I studied neuropsychology and pediatric neurology, did rounds in pediatric endocrinology, and dabbled in genetics by auditing the course at the medical school. When that was over, I was somewhat acquainted with a third eighth of the elephant– the biological bases of learning and behavioral problems. However, I wished I had known more about temperament, attention deficit disorder, hormonal problems, neurological disorders, and other biological influences on behavior seventeen years earlier when I had started my career as a educator.

Having to get back to work and missing the beach, I took a job as a visiting professor at the University of Hawaii, where I assisted the faculty to develop a program for teachers of students with emotional and behavioral problems. It was my first time teaching primarily Asian Pacific Island American students. Again I was surprised by the learning styles of this new group of students. Two examples. I love to teach by class discussions. That turned out to be very difficult. Most of the students resisted any discussion of controversial topics because they were too polite to disagree with each other, because they did not wish to share their opinions with others in public, and because they were even more concerned than white students about saying something that the professor would disagree with. (Oh how I longed for those exciting confrontations in Tuskegee. I guess that is one of my prejudices.) The only thing that was more difficult than getting the students to express their opinions was to persuade them to ask questions or to say that they didn't understand something. "Anyone have any questions," I'd ask. One or two Haoulis (whites) would raise a hand. "Anyone not understand what I said?" Again only the Haoulis would raise their hands. During the third class, I presented some concepts that had always been difficult for students. This was a test. Again, not a single Asian Pacific Island American raised a hand. Aha! I knew something was different. Instead of asking the students whether they understood what I had said, I asked individual students to explain what they had learned. Bingo! Quite a few couldn't do so. Also, instead of asking students to raise their hands if they didn't understand something, I asked them to raise their hands if they understood what I had said. Revising the question paid off. Quite a few students didn't raise their hands.

As I had done in Tuskegee, and would continue to do wherever I taught, I had the students visit the local programs for young people with emotional and behavioral problems. I made sure to accompany them on the visit to the state hospital for the emotionally disturbed and developmentally disabled. I saw the same horrendous conditions I had seen elsewhere, except the patients' ethnic background was different. In Hawaii, the over-represented groups were poor children from Hawaiian American, other Micronesian Island American and Portuguese American backgrounds.

I left Hawaii at the end of the academic year and made my home base in the San Francisco Bay area. I had no job awaiting me, but that was not a problem. I had become an acknowledged expert in the education of students with emotional and behavioral problems after the publication of my first book. The publication of my second book, *Nine Rotten Lousy Kids*, which described the Phoenix School, had made my name known in the corrections field. It was easy for me to find work.

All told, I taught at six predominately white universities in the San Francisco Bay area, while periodically escaping to other countries to teach and live. I taught Latino students in Peru, Ecuador, Mexico, Nicaragua, and Costa Rica, and African students in Malawi and Ghana. I also visited education programs in many other countries in Africa, Asia, and Latin America. The next section describes some of the things I learned while working and traveling abroad.

Chapter 5

AFRICA, ASIA, AND LATIN AMERICA

M Y MOST SALIENT IMPRESSION, the one thing that stands out and comes to mind most often about education for emotionally disturbed and behavior disordered children and youth in developing countries, is the shocking difference between the programs that are administered and staffed by committed people who want to help children and those that serve as warehouses.

For example, the patients in the government-run hospital I visited in Ghana were almost all zonked out on massive doses of drugs. Almost all of them were either asleep in their beds or sitting out in the hot sun like zombies. There were no activities for them, no equipment, no therapy. When I asked the staff why the patients were over medicated, I was told that the staff had no way of measuring how much medication was in the patients' blood streams because they had no laboratory. And even if they had a laboratory, they still would have to sedate the patients because they did not have enough staff members to supervise patients who were not zonked out.

In the mental hospital in Malawi, fewer patients were knocked out on drugs, but those that were not, were left to wander around a fenced-in yard with no equipment or supervision. Children were left in the care of adult patients who were too disturbed to take care of them and who often abused them. Many of the children had removed the few tattered clothes they had and were wandering around naked through an empty yard. Treatment plans consisted of deciding which of three medications to give each person. As in Ghana, they had no facilities for determining the amount of medication circulating in a patient's bloodstream. Children with epilepsy were heavily scarred around the face and head because they were not provided with any type of headgear to protect them when they fell unconscious.

Neither program offered "patients" an education or any services that would have been appropriate for children or adolescents. For all practical purposes, they were treated as adults.

The charitable, private facilities I observed in Ghana and Malawi were far superior. Although they contained little in the way of high-tech equipment, they had locally produced furniture and teacher-made teaching materials. The children were not over medicated. They were well supervised. And they were taught by teachers who cared a great deal about their welfare.

Asia was no different. During a trip to China, I was very interested in visiting governmental programs for orphans and children with disabilities. However, because a number of reports about the scandalous conditions in Chinese institutions had been widely circulated in the United States only months before, the government had put such programs off-limits to foreign tourists. Fortunately, I connected with a savvy guide, who brought me to a program on Saturday when the administrators of the institution were off duty. As a result, he was able to talk our way inside.

Conditions in this particular welfare institution were terrible. The children seemed neglected and rejected. Actually, they seemed abandoned. The infants and toddlers were in cribs. The older children were grouped together in a few large rooms. No adults were attending them. There were no toys or materials for them to play with. There was absolutely nothing for them to do. Most of them sat or lay, quiet and motionless, on benches along the walls or on the floor. A few rocked silently or stimulated themselves by murmuring or waving their hands. The most severely developmentally disabled or emotionally disturbed children were strapped to potty chairs. The bottoms of their pants were open so that they could relieve themselves without soiling their clothes.

I'm glad our guide took us to a private facility run by a woman who was studying special education in Shanghai. The day we visited, the children were engaged in a school-wide special olympics program. Just about all of the children were participating, regardless of their disabilities. They were smiling and laughing and having a good time. The classrooms were inviting, bright, clean, and well supplied with homemade educational, rehabilitative, and recreational materials and a few pieces of manufactured equipment that had been secured for the children by people from abroad who had visited the program.

The appalling government-run "programs" in Africa, Latin America, and Asia remined me of some of the state hospital programs I saw in the United States in the 1960s and 70s. Fortunately, those programs have been eliminated in the United States. However, I continue to see governmental programs for students with emotional and behavioral problems in which control and management, not education and rehabilitation, are the primary goals of uncaring adults whose principle desire is to make the job as easy as possible for themselves.

The contrast overseas between the special education programs in urban and rural areas was almost as disturbing. For the most part, special education programs were practically non-existent in rural areas. And those that did exist were "financed" by the government and even less adequate than those in urban areas. Rural special education programs in the United States are funded infinitely better than those in developing countries. However, the difference between urban and rural special education programs still exists. In the United States, although rural students with disabilities account for less than 30 percent of the total population, they constitute the majority of unserved or under served students and their drop-out rate is 50 percent higher than the national average for all students with disabilities.

Another important way I profited professionally from working abroad was learning more about the influential role cultural factors play in education. For example, I experienced first hand how students learn in a non-competitive environment. At the outset of a meeting I was conducting in Peru with the second-year graduate students about their masters theses, I was interrupted by a student even before I had begun to present the information I thought they needed. "Dr. Grossman," she said in Spanish. "I think the first thing we should do is choose who we will write our theses with."

I looked over to my Peruvian counterpart for assistance. He agreed with her. In Peru, students worked on theses together, just as they did on most things. Actually, one of the 20 students risked her peers' disapproval by deciding to work on her thesis independently.

It was inspiring to see how well the students worked together. For example, if a student missed class, someone would ask for an extra copy of the handouts for the student, deliver it, and make sure the person also got the notes and was told about any announcements.

The program required the students to spend four mornings a week under the supervision of faculty at the school for children and adolescents with emotional and cognitive disabilities. I was amazed to see the extent to which the teachers and the teachers-in-training involved their students in group activities' despite their cognitive and emotional problems. I had never and still have never seen that amount of cooperative learning in any program in the United States.

The African teachers-in-training I taught in Malawi went one step further than the Peruvians. They chose a class leader who collected material for absent students, made sure everyone received copies of notes they missed, informed professors of the reasons why students missed class or came late, et cetera. In both countries, and in many others as well, students who had difficulty grasping some of the work were actively invited into study groups, unlike what sometimes happens in the United States, where such students are often excluded because they might not be able to contribute anything to the group. Marking on the curve was unheard of. It would have been impossible to get the students to accept a grading system in which their grades depended on how much better or worse they did in comparison to the others in the class. That does not foster cooperative learning.

We should learn from the more cooperative cultures in Latin America and Africa. We should stress cooperation rather than competition with our students, especially in special education programs where students in the same program have such a range of disabling conditions.

Another thing I learned about Latinos while teaching in Latin America, which I also observed later in the United States, is that in comparison to European Americans, Latinos tend to believe that children's behavior problems are caused by willfulness or stubbornness rather than emotional conflicts, intense emotions, unconscious motivation, and the like. Believing that children who misbehave are generally unwilling, not unable to control their behavior, Latino teachers tend to over-use positive and negative reinforcements to convince them to control themselves.

My students in Latin America had considerable difficulty with approaches for helping children deal with emotional problems that did not involve positive or negative reinforcements. Encouraging, cajoling, and coaxing the teachers-in-training to use cognitive techniques, life space interviewing, gradual desensitization, self management, and the like were ineffective with many of them. I had to resort to requiring them to use such techniques (as I had done in the correctional facilities in California). Only after I had required them to use the techniques and they saw for themselves that the techniques were effective, were they able to reduce their use of consequences.

In this country, many Latinos, and for that matter many people from a variety of ethnic backgrounds, (you may be one of them) discount the roles that emotional conflicts, intense emotions, and unconscious motivation play in our lives. As a result, they tend to use only behavioral techniques with their emotionally and behavior-disordered students. In fact, I am dismayed to say, there are still many professionals, including professors, who deny the value of using the word "emotion" when thinking about or planning for the students we are discussing.

Many of the parents I worked with in Latin America, especially those from rural areas and those with little education, had little scientific understanding of the causes of their children's disabilities. Many of them believed that their children were born with disabilities because God was punishing them through their children for their bad behavior, because they had done something to someone who had used some magical power to get even with them, et cetera. Believing that their children's disabilities were the wish of God, they did not want to thwart God's desires by attempting to change their children's conditions. (On the other hand, these parents tended to be very accepting of their children's disabilities and very devoted, caring, and loving.)

Many parents who did not share these beliefs were not disposed to secure special education services for their children because they were unaware of its potential benefits. Coming from rural areas and lacking education and exposure to special education, they had no reason to think that their children could improve.

I remember visiting a graduate of our program in Peru in

the small city in the rain forest where she had just initiated the first special education program for students with emotional and cognitive disabilities. She only had five students in her program. She had been working very diligently with a number of parents, but most of them were still unwilling to allow their children to go to school.

While such beliefs are much much less prevalent among Latinos in the United States, they are far from extinct, especially among immigrant parents who had little or no exposure to special education in their countries of origin. They also can be found among immigrants from other parts of the world and among some religious European Americans as well.

While I was in Malawi, a teacher-in-training described the peculiar behavior of a boy in the village where he had been teaching. He believed the boy was acting that way because his father was seriously abusing him. What should he do about the situation, he asked. Being new to the country and unfamiliar with the culture, I naturally turned the question back to the class, but no one offered any suggestions. I contributed two possibilities solutions. One solution involved talking to and working with the father. The teacher said that he couldn't intrude in family matters in his culture. Almost all of the 40 teachers in the class agreed. Someone suggested asking the chief to talk to the father. The teacher rejected that suggestion because it, too, would be meddling in someone else's business. The vast majority of the teachers agreed with him.

Then I offered my second suggestion. I described my research about children who had resisted their parents' physical, psychological, or sexual abuse and said that perhaps he could try to get the boy to do the same. That caused a small uproar in the class. "No, no", some teachers shouted. It would not be proper to teach the boy to be disrespectful to his father even in those circumstances. Again the majority agreed.

We spent the remainder of the period talking about two themes: African solutions to the problem at hand and the cultural inappropriateness of many of the things they were being taught by the American professors who were preparing them to become special educators in Africa. (I should mention that this was true despite the fact that five of the seven American professors were African Americans.)

One final example of the cultural differences I experienced. Working and traveling in Africa, Asia, and Latin America made me realize that the fast-paced and rigidly scheduled way things tend to be organized in the United States and some other highly developed countries is not the way things are done in most of the world. The parties, dances, and other social events I attended in Latin America and Africa started hours after they were "scheduled" to begin. Meetings usually began a half hour to an hour after their announced times, and classes commenced within 15 minutes or so of the time they were slated for.

In many developing areas where the transportation facilities were limited and phones were rare, it was not unusual for people to miss a scheduled meeting entirely because of unforeseen circumstances. At times, the start of the university academic year was postponed for weeks or months. Students sometimes arrived for the start of the semester weeks late, as did paychecks.

While I was teaching in Peru, the university was two and a half years behind "schedule." That meant that students had to wait that long after graduating from high school and being accepted into the university to begin their studies. In Ghana, the delay was only one year.

In addition, the pace of life is much more relaxed in the developing world. People are calmer and enjoy their time more. It's not a big deal if things aren't completed on time. In fact, that's often the expectation. "On time" is a flexible concept. No wonder in the United States many students of color and their parents have difficulty adjusting and adhering to the concept of time that exists in our school systems and teacher training programs.

Living and traveling abroad added a fourth eighth of the elephant–culturally and contextually appropriate approaches to emotional and behavioral problems.

Chapter 6

GENDER ISSUES

DURING THE LATTER PART OF MY CAREER, my interest in gender issues in education intensified. I wanted to learn the answer to four questions: Are there gender differences in the way students function in school? If so, what are the causes of these differences? Do teachers treat males and females differently? And, do male and female teachers and professors have different instructional and classroom management styles? I began by observing and questioning the teachers I supervised and reading the literature. Eventually, I got involved in some original research. When I finished, my wife and I wrote a book, *Gender Issues in Education,* that presented what we had learned about the fifth eighth of the elephant. (1) In general, I concluded that there are significant gender differences in the ways students function in school. There are also gender differences in the ways male and female teachers instruct students, in the kinds of student behaviors teachers encourage and accept, whether they perceive students' behaviors as a problem and how they handle "problem" behavior. I also found that male and female professors have somewhat different ideas about the best way to handle problem behavior. (2) I did not reach closure about the origin of most gender differences because there still is too little research to reach scientific conclusions about their causes.

In this section I will briefly discuss only what I learned about how these gender differences affect the education of students with behavior problems. One of the main questions I had was whether teachers use the same or different classroom-management techniques when they think students have misbehaved. I found that teachers tend to reprimand males more often than females. They tend to speak softly and privately to girls, but publicly and harshly to boys. With younger children, they tend to use physical methods like poking, slapping, grabbing, pushing, squeezing, and so on with boys and negative comments, or disapproving gestures, and other forms of non-verbal communication with girls.

Public and harsh reprimands and physical forms of discipline and severe punishments can cause students to react rebelliously to punishments that they feel are too harsh for their "crimes" and cause them to be referred to special education. Thus, these differences may also contribute to the over representation of males, especially African American males, in programs for students with emotional and behavioral problems.

Do this exercise; you might find it interesting. A teacher is emerging from a school building on to the playground where he/she has recess or lunch duty. Suddenly, the teacher hears shouts, "Fight, fight, they're fighting" and sees students running towards the far corner of the yard. The teacher pushes through the throng of children and sees a familiar sight. Two boys, ages seven to 14 (you pick their ages), are fighting. The school bully, who makes life as miserable as he can for the weak kids, is beating up on the school scapegoat, who never defends himself against the verbal and physical abuse that is hurled his way.

Now, imagine that you are the teacher. Who are you more upset, angry, or frustrated with? Is it the bully who picks on the weak kids or the scapegoat who never defends himself? No cop outs. No saying you're equally upset at both of them. Close your eyes; visualize the scene; and don't open them until you've made a decision. Have you reached a decision?

If not, close your eyes. You can read on if you have made a choice.

This is what I have discovered about students' choices after using this exercise in my courses for 35 years. With numerous exceptions, male, working class, and African American and Latino students are more likely to be upset, angry, or frustrated with the scapegoat. Female, middle class, and European-American undergraduate and graduate students are comparatively more upset by the bully.

Having grasped the situation, the teacher takes action. If the teacher is female, or middle class, or white, he or she is likely to start on the bully. "Don't you know . . . How dare you hit . . . You cannot . . . I'm going to have to . . . et cetera."

On the other hand, if the teacher is male, or working class or African American, and especially if he is all three, the teacher is likely to focus on the scapegoat. "Why don't you . . . Can't you . . . If you don't start defending yourself . . . et cetera."

Did the prediction hold up for you?

A second question I investigated was why females account for only between 12 and 16 percent of the students in programs for students with emotional problems. I concluded that the answer was not that males have more emotional problems than females. On the contrary, there is evidence that females have as many if not more emotional problems than males. School-age girls are more fearful and anxious than boys and are also more likely than boys to experience sadness or depression.

The answer lies in the referral process. Teachers are much more likely to refer males than females to special education programs for students with emotional and behavioral disorders. Here's why.

The vast majority of teachers who are in a position to refer students to special education are female. While all teachers want their students to be well behaved, female teachers typically are less tolerant of "male pattern disruptive" behavior. They prefer cooperative, rather than competitive, behavior and compliant, rather than assertive, behavior.

Female students with emotional problems act out less than males. They are more likely to show signs of depression, fear, and anxiety, while males are more likely to act out their anger. (These generalizations are least likely to apply to African American females.) Girls with emotional problems are more likely to appear timid and withdrawn, while boys tend to act assertively and aggressively and to do so more intensely. (Actually, while girls commit less-overt aggression than boys, they engage in more- covert aggression.)

The behavior that is most likely to call a teacher's attention to students' emotional problems are acting out, disruptive, externalizing behaviors that are typically characteristic of angry, resentful, jealous, and rebellious students and male students. Withdrawal, and internalizing behaviors that are more like to characterize anxious, fearful, and especially depressed students and female students, are much less likely to provoke responses from teachers. Thus, female teachers are less attentive to and more accepting of the symptoms of their female students' emotional problems and they are less likely to refer the females to special education.

Chapter 7

TEACHERS AND PROFESSORS

I HAVE MET MANY DEDICATED TEACHERS, teachers-in-training, and professors who are committed to adapting their approaches to emotional and behavioral problems to the diverse characteristics of students. However, in general, the field is very far from attaining this goal. One reason for this is that there are not enough teachers from non-middle-class or non-European-American backgrounds.

Although only 68 percent of all elementary and secondary school students are European Americans, 87 percent of regular-education teachers are European Americans. The corresponding figures for African American, Latino, and Asian Pacific Island American students and teachers are 16 percent versus 8 percent, 12 percent versus 2 percent, and 3 percent versus 2 percent respectively. (1)

Special educators are also not representative of the students they teach. (2) Teachers from poor, non-middle-class or non-European-American backgrounds are increasingly scarce. Although 32 percent of students in special education programs are non-European Americans, only 6.6 percent of special education teachers are African Americans, only 3.1 percent are Latinos, and fewer than 2 percent are Asian Pacific Island Americans or Native Americans.

My experience leads me to believe that the over representation of middle-class European-American regular and special educators is a disastrous situation. Most of the middle-class European-American teachers I have taught or known do not really understand non-middle-class, non-European

American students. And many of them do not value a multicultural approach to classroom management. I have heard them use many arguments to justify their position. I'll discuss the two that, in my experience, are the most common.

All people are basically the same so they should be treated the same. Treating some students differently than others is discriminatory.

I disagree, of course. Human beings are basically the same. They prefer success to failure, praise and recognition to criticism or condemnation, and acceptance and attention to rejection and inattention. However, peoples' behaviors in these situations are influenced by different cultural veneers. They have different criteria for success. They find different forms of praise and recognition rewarding. They differ in terms of when, where, why, and how they are willing to accept criticism or condemnation. And they express acceptance and rejection in their own culturally determined ways. Therefore, if teachers expect all individuals to behave the same way or interpret everyone's behavior from a single culturally determined point of view, they may fail to respond to the unique needs of many of their students.

In addition, the result of treating all students with emotional and behavioral problems the same may be that those who do not fit the model used by their teachers are treated in a discriminatory manner. Educators who believe that providing students the same instructional techniques, classroom-management approaches, and so on have the mistaken notion that they are treating them equally and being fair to them. However, they are not treating all students the same, but are dealing with some students in a culturally appropriate manner and others in a biased manner. There is a more valid way of treating students the same, which is to provide all students with culturally appropriate educational approaches. This may make it appear that students are being treated differently; however they are actually being treated the same– in a non-discriminatory manner.

It is impossible to accommodate educational approaches to the needs of the many ethnic groups found in any particular school system or often within a particular classroom.

This is incorrect. It's not true that every culture requires a unique educational approach. The alternative methods of managing students, organizing classrooms, and so on are limited. For example, educators can encourage or require their students to work individually or in groups; they can motivate them through the use of competitive games or cooperative settings; they can allow them to work at their own pace or encourage them to work as quickly as possible; they can attempt to develop close personal relationships with them or maintain a "professional distance;" and they can correct and criticize them in front of their peers or privately. Since educators are choosing between alternatives as limited as those listed above, they can easily adapt their methodology to the cultural needs of their students.

In general, but with many exceptions, when the European American teachers-in-training who devalue multicultural approaches graduate from their education-preparation programs, their attitudes persist. They are neither prepared for nor committed to serving the diverse needs of students with emotional and behavioral problems. The European American graduates of my programs are only partial exceptions to this generalization. They tend to change their attitudes about multicultural approaches, but many of them demonstrate a less-than-total commitment to implementing what they have learned.

One of the ways I measure the effectiveness of the courses in diversity that I teach is to compare my students' responses at the outset and at the end of the semester to questions about how they think a variety of problematic classroom situations should be handled. When I do so, I find that at the end of the course they are much more likely to believe that teachers should adapt to their students' individual characteristics those techniques they use to deal with emotional and behavioral problems. However, when I ask my students if they would actually make these adaptations, their answers are mixed. In general, they report that they have adapted or anticipate adapting many of their instructional techniques to their students' cultural, socioeconomic, contextual, and linguistic needs. That is unlikely to cause them problems. However, they are less willing to adjust their classroom management approaches to their students' individual needs because accepting certain kinds of behavior would make them very uncomfortable and could cause problems with their colleagues and administrators.

Having been asked to leave my first full-time university teaching job because I had adapted the instructional and classroom-management approaches in the lab school to the needs of the African American students in the program, I know that the threat they experience is real. So, I try to strike a balance between encouraging my students to take risks and discussing strategies that they can use to challenge the system without paying the price I paid when I was young, inexperienced, and naive.

Teacher educators bear much of the responsibility for the lack of diversity among our teachers. During my thirty-some years in higher education, I have known some outstanding European American professors who were dedicated to preparing their students to succeed with all children and concerned about achieving diversity in their teacher training programs. However, in general, most European American professors are doing little to remedy this situation because they are not very interested in diversity issues. With some exceptions, they do not attempt to recruit non-middle-class and non-European American students into their preparation programs. When they do recruit them, they tend to choose students who, like themselves, have adopted a middle-class

European American way of life. And they often turn off many of the students who have not assimilated to the mainstream culture by using culturally and contextually inappropriate instructional, classroom-management, and assessment approaches in their classes. The overrepresentation of middle-class European American teachers in our schools is unlikely to improve until these professors intensify their recruitment efforts among non-middle class and non-European American students, adapt their methods to these students, and make their programs more relevant to them.

The situation in the university where I taught for many years is a good example. A number of my colleagues, who were awarded federal funds to provide scholarships to "minority" and/or bilingual students in order to increase the number of non-European American and bilingual educators, asked me what I did to recruit students for the programs I ran. I told them that we sent letters to the more than one thousand school buildings in our service area, made presentations about our program in the local school districts and at meetings of the county education administrators, interviewed candidates at sites off campus that were convenient to their places of residence or work, followed up every inquiry with at least a telephone call, asked graduates of our program to contact prospective students to encourage them to apply, and so on. They thanked me, but implemented few, if any, of my suggestions. The result in many cases was that their minimal recruitment efforts were unsuccessful.

Professors who teach behavior-management courses and courses about students with emotional and behavioral problems also bear much of the responsibility for the fact that their graduates are not prepared to serve the needs of our diverse student population. Professors do not model a flexible management approach. Moreover, they train their students to use the behavior-management approaches that make them, the professors, most comfortable, the ones that

fit the professors' own ethnic and socioeconomic backgrounds. (3)

I have to admit that my professor's heart was not pure
either. I too taught my students to use approaches that I
preferred. It began during my first year as a full-time professor, 1966, and lasted for almost ten years. I'd like to
claim that I was naive at the time. However, the truth is
that I was prejudiced.

My first year as a full-time professor coincided with the
first annual conference of directors of programs for students
with serious emotional problems sponsored by the federal
government. I attended every single conference that was
held during the next five or so years. Attending these con-
ferences, I met many people who thought like me and
became friendly with some of the authors of publications that
had been extremely helpful to me while I was learning to be
a good teacher. I also met many professors whose ideas
about how to help students, with emotional and behavioral
problems were very different from mine. I can still recall the
first time I became aware that we did not all agree. It
occurred during the first few minutes of our first meeting.
We went around the room introducing ourselves and telling
the others which program we directed. I said that I was in
charge of the program for teachers of emotionally disturbed
students, as did most professors. However, quite a few professors announced with a special emphasis that their programs were for teachers of students with behavior disorders.
Professors who emphasized behaviorist approaches said that
their programs were for students with behavior disorders.
Those who favored a more psychodynamic approach called
the students emotionally disturbed. We had common inter-
ests as program directors, but we also thought very differently about how to help students.

In those days, it was fairly common at professional confer-
ences to pair a psychodynamic-oriented professor with a

behaviorist and let them debate their viewpoints or discuss some students from their different perspectives. If I hadn't been so cocksure that the psychodynamic approach was the end-all and so set against using extrinsic consequences with students, I would have been more open to behavioristic approaches. Unfortunately, it was too easy for me to go along with the trend of the day.

How silly it was. Neither school of thought was right. Talk about the blind men and the elephant. They both included some of the truth and both were insufficient by themselves. They were complementary approaches, not alternative approaches. How prejudiced I was at the time. I had definitely fallen into the trap of belonging to a camp. We were right; they were wrong. We knew how to help kids; they didn't. I had prejudged behaviorism and, as I said, I would not be open to it for quite some time. In fact, even now I am not too enamored of it.

For many years, I directed a bilingual/multicultural education personnel-preparation program. Many times, students would complain angrily to me that they felt that they were studying in two different programs. The faculty who taught their courses in the bilingual/multicultural program were teaching them how to adapt their methodology to the ethnic, socioeconomic class, gender, contextual, and linguistic differences among students. However, diversity was seldom mentioned in their regular education courses, in which they were being taught that one method fits all students.

Unfortunately professors are not doing what is necessary to improve their ability to prepare educators to meet the challenges of our diverse society. The last time I attended a national education conference, I made it a point to attend as many sessions that dealt with diversity as possible. What I saw was consistent and unfortunate: African American, Asian Pacific Island American, and Latino professors presenting to other African American, Asian Pacific Island

American, and Latino professors and teachers. The situation had not changed very much since the 1960s. The people who had the greatest need to attend the sessions were elsewhere, participating in sessions that did not deal with diversity and that were presented by European American professors.

I have observed somewhat the same principle at work regarding my most recent book about behavior problems. When I wrote the second edition, I added more about multicultural approaches to what I had included in the first edition, so much more, that we changed the title from *Trouble Free Teaching* to *Classroom Behavior Management in a Diverse Society.* (4) When the second edition went to press, I asked my editor how he thought it would do. "We should double or triple the sales," he replied. Wrong! The additional multicultural emphasis lowered sales. Apparently, some of the professors who might otherwise have adopted the book were put off by diversity issues.

A couple of years ago I went to a conference that was attended by many of the thousand or so professors who had received a desk copy of the book. I asked the professors I was acquainted with what they thought of the books they had received. The professors of color and the few European American professors who were particularly interested in diversity issues made very positive comments about the book. However, the comments of the majority of the European American professors indicated that they hadn't even reviewed it.

The comments of two professors of color were especially enlightening. They told me that at their university, faculty committees chose the textbooks for the courses they taught. Although they both had recommended my book to the committees, the majority of the committee members (European American professors) had rejected their suggestions–sometimes rather adamantly.

Fortunately, I have two much-more-positive experiences to report. The first occurred a number of years ago while I was attending a conference of the Council for Children with Behavior Disorders. I was in a hotel lounge talking to three other professors. We four were all that remained of a large group of professors who had been talking the night away. I realized that I felt a real affinity for them, and that they each had described how they had been fired, asked to leave, or denied tenure at least once while they were classroom teachers or professors.

That night I learned that professors who really want to help all students should be prepared to experience the anger of their colleagues and administration and to pay the price for bucking the system. Most, but certainly not all, of the professors that I have known who were ready to pay the price were non-European Americans. The three professors I just discussed however, were all committed, middle-class European Americans.

The second happened just a few months ago just when I was feeling particularly discouraged about the sales of *Classroom Behavior Management in a Diverse Society*. Out of the clear blue sky, I received a call from a professor inviting me to be the instructor/consultant of an internet workshop his university was co-sponsoring on diversity issues in working with students with emotional and behavioral problems. They had picked me because of the diversity content of my publications. How pleased I was to hear that, and how excited I became about the opportunity to share my ideas with participants from around the country. I got busy preparing the material I wanted people to read. This book is an expanded version of the material. I learned a lesson. You never know who will hear or read your ideas and what kind of impact they may have. Now I feel rejuvenated and can end this book on a more optimistic note.

In 1957, when I started teaching students with emotional

and behavioral problems, I knew very little of what I needed to know in order to succeed with them. The field was so new that research results about the most effective ways of working with these students were extremely scarce. When I started teaching, I didn't even realize that I needed information about how to work with a diverse group of students. I knew nothing about and thought nothing about diversity issues. Most professors and researchers were no different. Words such as African American, Asian Pacific Island American, Latino, culture, ethnicity, prejudice, bias, discrimination, gender, socioeconomic class, et cetera, did not appear in the literature or in the lectures of the vast majority of professors.

I have changed, and as a result I have had a glimpse of five eighths of the elephant. The field has also changed. Our scientific knowledge about how to deal with students with emotional and behavioral problems has expanded dramatically. In addition, our mission statements now include goals for meeting students' diverse needs. Today, you can find the diversity-related words listed above in the education literature. I have some reason to hope that they will soon appear more frequently in the indexes of the classroom-management textbooks teachers-in-training read and in the lectures they hear.

NOTES

Chapter 1

1. Grossman, H. 1966. *Teaching the Emotionally Disturbed: A Casebook.* New York: Holt, Rinehart, & Winston.

Chapter 2

1. This book describes the program.
   Grossman, H. (1972). *Nine Rotten Lousy Kids.* New York: Holt, Rinehart & Winston.
2. Patton, J. M. 1981. *A Critique of Externally Oriented Behavior Management Approaches as Applied to Black Children.* ERIC ED 204-209.
3. Kochman, T. 1981. *Black and White Styles in Conflict.* Chicago: University of Chicago Press. 117.
4. Grossman, H. 1995. *Educating Hispanic Students: Cultural Implications for Instruction, Classroom Management, Counseling and Assessment.* Springfield, IL: Charles C Thomas. p. 104.
5. Ewing, N. J. 1994. Restructuring teacher education for inclusiveness: A dream deferred for African American children. In *Effective Education for African American Exceptional Learners,* eds B.A. Ford, F.E. Obiakor, and J.E. Patton, 198-199. Austin, TX: Pro-ed.

Chapter 3

1. *60 Minutes* September 26, 1999.

Chapter 6

1. Grossman, H., & Grossman, S. H. 1994. *Gender Issues in Education.* Boston: Allyn & Bacon.
2. Research on gender differences can be found in the following references: Grossman, H., & Grossman, S. H. 1994. *Gender*

Issues in Education. Boston: Allyn & Bacon.

Grossman, H. 1994. *Professors' Preferences for Classroom/Behavior Management Techniques: Consensus and Ethnic, Gender, and Socioeconomic Class Differences.* ERIC ED 364-537.

Grossman, H. 1995. *Special Education in a Diverse Society.* Boston: Allyn & Bacon. Chapters 1, 7, and 8.

Chapter 7

1. Grossman, H. 1998. *Achieving Educational Equality: Assuring All Students an Equal Opportunity in School.* Springfield, IL: Charles C. Thomas. Chapter 17.

2. Grossman, H. 1998. *Ending Discrimination in Special Education.* Springfield, IL: Charles C Thomas. Chapter 4.

3. Grossman, H. 1994. *Professors' Preferences for Classroom/Behavior Management Techniques: Consensus and Ethnic, Gender, and Socioeconomic Class Differences.* ERIC ED 364-537.

4. Grossman, H. 1995. *Classroom Behavior Management in a Diverse Society.* 2nd Ed. Mountain View, CA: Mayfield.